MORE ADVANCE PRAISE

A Circle of Men

"Custom-organizing a men's support group is inevitably a do-it-yourself project. Bill Kauth's *A Circle of Men* is by far the most detailed and comprehensive manual on the subject—providing time-tested advice seasoned with good humor."
—Christopher Harding, Ph.D., editor of *Wingspan: Journal of the Male Spirit*

"A practical companion for *any* men's group. *A Circle of Men* is a valuable resource that will help promote the development of a vital, nurturing, and healthy new male community."
—Aaron R. Kipnis, Ph.D., author of *Knights Without Armor*

"Bill Kauth has done the work—with men in the field and now in this most helpful book. Trust this man. Kauth walks his talk. This jewel of a book provides readers with the benefit of years of hard work and the sweat of hundreds of men. Even if you are not in a men's group, read *A Circle of Men* to find out more about yourself as a man or your men friends."
—Shepherd Bliss, Ph.D., Professor of Men's Studies at JFK University and Literary Director of The Sons of Orpheus: A Men's Mythopoetic Community

"Bill Kauth's contribution to the how-tos of male group-building is longstanding. He has written *A Circle of Men* in a readable style and organized it as a practical guidebook for the furthering of men's work. I strongly recommend it."
—Douglas Gillette, author (with Robert Moore) of *King, Warrior, Magician, Lover*

"Bill Kauth's book is a blessing. His experience, insight, and clarity will assist and inspire men from all walks of life."
—Ralph Blum, author of *The Book of Runes*

"An excellent resource for any man wanting to start a men's group. This book provides structure, support, and vision for creating *A Circle of Men*."
—James Sniechowski, founder of The Menswork Center, Los Angeles

"If you're looking to start your own men's group, an excellent resource is *A Circle of Men*. Author Bill Kauth, a cofounder of the popular New Warrior Training™, explains how to create a group for friendship, community, and intimacy. The book includes chapters on choosing group members, suggested formats for the first eight meetings, the use of ritual, and the role of physical touch."
—*New Age Journal*

ROGER C. EHLERT, Ph.D.
1802 N. 15th STREET
COEUR D'ALENE, IDAHO 83814

A Circle of Men

THE ORIGINAL MANUAL FOR MEN'S SUPPORT GROUPS

BILL KAUTH, M.S.

ST. MARTIN'S PRESS
NEW YORK

A CIRCLE OF MEN: THE ORIGINAL MANUAL FOR MEN'S SUPPORT GROUPS. Copyright © 1992 by Human Development Associates, Inc. All rights reserved. Printed in the United States of America. No part of this book may be used or reproduced in any manner whatsoever without written permission except in the case of brief quotations embodied in critical articles or reviews. For information, address St. Martin's Press, 175 Fifth Avenue, New York, N.Y. 10010.

Editor: Jared Kieling
Design by Robert Bull Design

Library of Congress Cataloging-in-Publication Data

Kauth, Bill
     A Circle of men : the original manual for men's support groups /
  Bill Kauth.
       p.   cm.
  ISBN 0-312-07247-3
  1. Social work with men—United States.   2. Social group work—
  United States.   3. Self-help groups—United States.   I. Title.
  HV1441.8.U5K38 1992
  362.8--dc20   91-41831
                                                          CIP

First Edition: May 1992

10 9 8 7 6 5 4 3 2 1

DEDICATED TO

Keith Anderson

The Men of "The Grandaddy of Them All" Men's Group (1972–75)
Perry, Bill, Walt, Mac, Steve, Keith, John, Marc, Paul, Tom,
Richard (a.k.a. Jim), Jay, and Jeff

and Onzie
Ever loyal and supportive friend, lover, wife, mentor, student, and sweetie

Other Acknowledgments:

Inspirational mentors:	Jack Gibb, Joseph Zinker, Dick Olney, Elam Nunnally, and Robert Bly
Spiritual guides:	Oscar Ichaso, Da Free John, David DuRovy, and Harry Palmer
Conceptual collaborators:	Bob Walters, Susan Evans
Supportive colleagues:	Ron Hering, Rich Tosi
Insightful suggestions:	Bob Porter, Clint Jessor, Asa Baber, David Lindgren, and Killian Kuntz
Brilliant design artist:	George Lottermoser
Playful cartoonist:	Dave Long
Devoted editors:	Lois Mercer, Jared Kieling, and The Folks Kauth

MEN'S WORK IN PROGRESS

This book is a dynamic, evolving process.
As I grow and learn, the book expands and changes.
At some point it has to be committed to paper.
So this book exists in its current printing, though unfinished form.
The next edition will reflect insights and developments of what works in groups for the conscious empowerment of men. I welcome any suggestions, corrections, or additions you may have.
Please write to me at the address below. Thanks.

Bill Kauth
c/o Human Development Associates, Inc.
4913 N. Newhall St.
Milwaukee, WI 53217

"It's a bunch of stuff my dad gave me. I'm going to go through it and save some, throw some away, and add some of my own."

CONTENTS

ACTIVITIES AND CHALLENGES FOR YOUR GROUP 59

SITUATIONS AND DYNAMICS IN YOUR GROUP 87

MEN'S READINGS AND INFORMATION 109

INTRODUCTION

Great . . . what's a men's group?

Who am I and why was this book written?

I want you to know some of my personal history, which will help you enjoy and understand my ideas on groups. It may serve to personalize and humanize this work if you can feel some of the struggles and delights along my path.

I was twenty-eight years old when I got my first taste of real "men's friends" and the feeling of community that had been missing from my life. As a fairly typical 1960s youth, I had been searching for that "something different." I didn't consciously know what it was, but I searched hard and long. I worked at jobs from cab driver to teacher, from salesman to social worker. I lived in other states, cities, and countries. I got involved in two fraternities, three political groups, social events, parties, dances, and various life-styles. Searching, looking, trying to find that real feeling of belonging and loving.

In 1971 I returned to the University of Wisconsin looking for new directions. Studying for my masters degree in educational psychology, I got some class experience in small group process. This led, in 1973, to an invitation by a friend to co-lead a men's group. His wife was involved in a women's group. He could see the powerful supportive value that it had for her and he wanted the same experience for himself.

I responded, "Great, let's do it. . . . what's a men's group?" We began, despite knowing little about support groups and absolutely nothing about men's groups. Fortunately, this did not seem to matter. Within weeks we began to experience the warm, inclusive feeling of "our group." Tuesday night was our "group night" and it rapidly became a sacrosanct time for everyone in the group. **Nothing** took precedence over my men's group.

I knew I liked "group" because it seemed that I often did not walk home — I floated! It was as if I was high from the experience of finding the loving, supportive friends and community I had been wanting through my early adulthood. I now had people (and men yet!) with whom I could really open up, share my fears and doubts, my joys and brags, and be supported and loved through it all. One Native American tribe I heard about calls such people "shoulder friends."

My wife also appreciated that I had this group because I was no longer totally dependent on her for nurturing and support. I also brought home new energy, delight, and power as I learned about qualities in myself I had not known or known well. My personal growth stimulated our growth as a couple. And within six months my wife had started a women's group for herself.

I got high. No drugs, no physical exertion, no new places, no meditative spaces. Just the joy of being with men and having the safety of enough loving acceptance to be myself.

That was the purpose of our group: to support and help one another in learning new ways to be—socially, personally, professionally, and in relation to each other. Group was a safe place to try out new behaviors such as being more assertive, relaxed, or confident. In group we could talk about unusually sensitive topics, like sex, fathers, and intimacy. We also developed socially and shared some beautiful times with pot-luck dinners, camping, and, of course, parties.

With my group being such a significant ongoing part of my life, I told others about it, and they often asked how they could have such a group. I didn't know of any place one could go to find what we had created. At that point, I was offered a job with a free-thinking social service organization that gave me the flexibility to experiment in organizing groups as alternatives to drug abuse. My group was such a high for me that I figured a similar process could work for others. Men's groups were becoming my driving passion.

Over the next three years (1974–77) I organized over 100 different groups. There were maybe a dozen more men's groups, lots and lots of women's groups, and many mixed groups. There were also some teenage groups, couples' groups, drug-users' groups, and a widows' group. We even attempted a shy people's group, for which no one showed up! (True story!)

Each of these groups was organized with two previously trained leaders (social workers, counselors). Most of the groups were highly successful, lasting two and three years and providing much learning and loving support for the members. Some were failures for reasons such as poor organization or inadequate leadership, things I learned painfully and did not repeat.

The need for well-trained leaders seemed obvious, so I developed a six-week-long training process for my volunteer group leaders. After running a half dozen group leadership training groups, I began to notice that these groups were **bonding** very quickly and in a specifically similar pattern. The pattern seemed to reflect the particular training skills I was teaching. I guessed that if these skills were taught to any group of reasonably receptive people, they would bond into a successful support group.

Over the next couple of years, using what I had learned, I put together a business organization that created situations for friendships to happen. I called this project Small World Groups, Inc. This totally new private enterprise would organize eight to twelve highly compatible people into a support group. Our clients paid us for organizing them and training them in many of the skills and ideas contained in this book. Everyone in each group was trained to be able to be the group leader. Thus we created "leaderful" support groups—as distinguished from "leaderless" (no leader) or "therapy groups" (one leader). We organized over thirty Small World groups.

It was a noble idea, clearly ahead of its time. I wanted to organize men's groups, but in 1979 nobody was interested. In fact the only type of group anyone was interested in was singles' groups. I learned a lot about how sexual tension in a mixed-sex group makes for a relatively short group life. Small World Groups was a flyer and it crashed. We starved to death financially.

As I was dusting myself off from that experiment in making a living at building community, I moved into doing psychotherapy full time, all the while staying aware of men's issues. In the early 1980s I also began educating myself on the plight of the planet, especially around the nuclear threat. My inner "little boy" who grew up scared in the duck-and-cover early 1950s longed for a planet safe from the Bomb. I became a peace activist, joining groups like the Mobilization for Survival and Beyond War.

Through it all I was looking to women for the answers. I was an active feminist. The women's movement had provided a unique awareness. I learned a lot from my women friends, and I attempted to identify with them to the point of calling myself a feminist therapist. What this meant to me was that I shared authentic, emotionally real relationships with my clients. And I was learning from feminists that it was men who controlled the bombs in missiles shaped like penises and men who had put the planet in danger. As a new peace activist, I bought it.

Deep inside me, somewhere down under my creative rationalizations, I knew that I was somehow selling out my own gender. There was something about being a man and proudly calling myself a feminist that was not congruent for me. Was I still trying to please women to get approval, get love, get laid, or what?

Then in May of 1982 the bombshell hit. *New Age* magazine published their landmark Robert Bly interview that gave men all across the country some desperately needed answers and focus. That ten-page article was copied and recopied and sent from man to man around the country thousands of times. To sum up what Robert Bly said in a couple of sentences: *Our dads weren't there for us, so we were all raised by women, and we can't learn about manhood from women, so we have to learn about manhood from each other.*

For two years I contained these obvious yet stunningly new ideas, allowing them to perk inside me. During this time I attended a powerful and dynamic training weekend called Understanding Yourself and Others. It was during this training that I confessed, between sobs, my embarrassing mission to end war and create a safe planet. The leaders said, "You can't end war out there until you end the war inside." I began to understand that men often use violence because they feel powerless. Empowering men was essential to a safe planet.

In 1983 I was invited to participate in the biannual Wisconsin Feminist Therapists' conference. As it turned out, of 125 feminist therapists, I was the only one with a penis (not that I checked real close). And I experienced something strange and new. Having been a feminist for years, I was used to groups like this one, and I had always felt some sense of being shunned and ostracized just because I was male. This time I felt fully accepted; there was a genuine feeling of interdependence. I concluded that this group of women had come full circle in their struggle to feel powerful and were now able to relate with compassion to those (men) whom they had thought to be the oppressor.

I was deeply impressed by the evolution of women that I had witnessed over the decade. At that moment all I could think of was: "Why doesn't somebody do something for men?" And the finger randomly pointing out began pointing back. I made a commitment to work to empower men toward creating a safe planet. I had found a passion deeper than my fear of commitment.

In 1984 I put together a team to create a men's training program. I chose Ron Hering, a university professor with a Ph.D. in curriculum and twenty-five years of personal-growth training experience. The third member was Rich Tosi, who brought to the team the hard edge of ten years in the U.S. Marine Corps and a unique level of personal authenticity.

As we studied the situation of men, we observed that there is no meaningful shared passage into manhood for men today, nor has there been one for several generations. As partners we decided it was time to create a meaningful training/rite of passage/initiatory experience for men.

We looked around the country for other men's training events. All we found besides Robert Bly's splendid conferences were Justin Sterling's "Men, Sex, and Power" workshops. Tosi and I immediately flew to California to participate and learn. What we learned was to value the hard and primal side of manhood. We also saw that a training event with 150 men was impersonal, something for which they compensated through the building of geographically based "support teams."

We learned from the writings and tapes of men's mentors like Robert Bly that, historically, men as hunter-gatherers and farmers knew who they were as men. Their sons spent many, many hours every day with their fathers, learning just by being together what manhood was about. Then the elders would formally induct the young men into the community of men. But as technology evolved, our great-grandfathers went from the rural, farming culture to the urban, industrial culture. Men moved from the farms to the cities and into meaningless and/or unfulfilling work.

This was a profoundly significant shift, because our work is such an important part of our identity. Unlike women, who are essentially internal, nurturing creatures, we men are essentially external, out in the world, building-and-developing creatures. We often define ourselves by our work. Meaningless work in the factory or office left our great-grandfathers with little or nothing to give to their sons, including quantity (vs. quality) time. Also to be considered is the impact of the wars in this century, which destroyed the "archetypal warrior" in men and left them spiritually dead. (For more on this see Chapter 30.)

This involuntary abandonment by fathers means that for several generations boys in our culture have been raised almost entirely by women. And women, simply because they are women, cannot teach boys about manhood. Without men there is no possibility of any rite of passage into manhood.

Therefore, we men, for several generations, have been losing our sense of what Michael Meade calls gender ground.

From these working ideas we began creating the New Warrior Training Adventure Men's Weekend. It is designed as an intense gender-learning rite of passage for adult males ready to move into manhood. The training itself proved to be so powerful that it often took men three to six months to integrate the new learning into their everyday lives. But we noticed that those men who stayed in regular supportive contact with other men were able to hold more of the learning, embellish it, and integrate it more quickly. So we created a two-month-long, weekly follow-up, which we simply called the "integration group."

The learning goes on. We have built dozens of integration groups around the country, from which have come more ideas that have found their way into this book. Through the creativity of men in these groups, my original support group training model has been refined and honed again and again.

"How can men be lonely? This is the golden age of information and communication technology!"

Thus, the ideas and step-by-step model for support groups contained in this book are the result of nearly eighteen years of observing, planning, organizing, experimenting, and developing men's groups. During this time **a process has emerged by which a group of men who are reasonably compatible and who come together with a mutuality of intention will learn rapidly to trust, love, resolve conflict, and care for each other.** Part of its beauty is its simplicity. The model is very simple to learn and use.

The one essential ingredient is a willingness to stay with your men's group and learn through being together. I call this **commitment** and it is the subject of the second chapter of this book. The ideas and techniques in this book work. The model can be used successfully by anyone honestly willing to use it. I encourage any man who believes he can make his life richer to dive in—make a commitment to yourself, organize your group, and begin making some wonderful changes in your life as you build your community. One of my mentors once said, **"The only way to have old friends is to make new friends."**

"A man doesn't have to live up to any narrow, societal image of manhood. There are many ancient images of men as healers, protectors, lovers, and partners with women, men, and nature. This is how we are in our depths: celebrators of life, ethical and strong."
—Aaron R. Kipnis, Ph.D., The New Male Manifesto,
Knights Without Armor

FOREWORD

How to use this book

This book is intended to guide you in knowing what kind of men's group you want, how to organize your group, and then, in detail, how to make **your** new group work.

This is a **programmed** textbook, which means it is designed to take you and your men's group **through** the steps necessary to create an enjoyable, purposeful, and long-lasting group experience. Many chapters contain work pages designed to be shared and used by the men of your group. These help to create norms and agreements to make the group run smoothly. The write-in work pages also increase mutual understanding, bring about the learning of skills, and serve as stimulators for new group experiences.

The book is made to be used, written in, and studied. It would be simple and useful for each man to have his own copy of this book from the start—not to mention a more solvent situation for the author. However, it has been quite deliberately published in a format that makes it possible to photocopy handout pages for all the men in your group.

If **you** intend to organize **your** own group and get it started, begin thinking now of yourself as the temporary group leader, because someone has to take that role for the first two or three meetings. Make the decision to be the leader and follow the steps in this book; it is easier than you may think, since your group will rapidly begin sharing the leadership.

The first chapter is an overview of modern socioeconomic history (early 1950s to the present). This will give you a feeling for why groups are such a powerful personal development tool for us in men's work.

Read Chapters 1 through 5 **before** beginning to organize your group. Once your group is organized and ready to start, re-read those chapters. Then focus on Chapter 6, to be fully prepared to start leading your first group meeting. From then on, follow the chapters through meetings 2 to 8. By then your group will be on its own.

Chapters 15 through 21 are made up of creative suggestions. If you think your group needs a boost or needs direction, check out the activities and challenges in these chapters. They range from brief learning exercises to developing a mission which could carry your group for years.

Chapters 22 through 28 comprise the troubleshooting section. If your group is stuck (or if you simply want to educate yourself more thoroughly about group process), read it.

The final Chapters 29 through 33 are intended to be thought-provoking, educational guideposts on your journey into enlightened manhood.

"We need to learn to love and be loved by the mature masculine. We need to learn to celebrate authentic masculine power and potency, not only for the sake of our personal well-being as men and for our relationships with others, but also because the crisis in mature masculinity feeds into the global crisis of survival we face as a species."

—Robert Moore and Douglas Gillette,
King, Warrior, Magician, Lover

PART ONE
ORGANIZING YOUR GROUP

"We need same sex friends because there are types of validation and acceptance that we receive only from our gendermates. There is much about our experience as men that can only be shared with, and understood by, other men. There are stories we can tell only to those who have wrestled in the dark with the same demons and been wounded by the same angels. Only men understand the secret fears that go with the territory of masculinity."

—Sam Keen, *Fire in the Belly*

WITH A LITTLE HELP FROM MY FRIENDS

The history and value of support groups

During the early years of the Beatles in the 1960s, there was a trend toward getting high through the use of drugs, especially hallucinogens such as marijuana and LSD. It was an experience of "higher consciousness" that millions of people wanted without the drugs! Millions succeeded through forms of meditation, healthy foods, jogging, biking, cross-country skiing, and **groups!**

The self-improvement support group is a fairly new phenomenon. Before the 1960s, support/growth groups were known only to the rich. Young women in posh finishing schools participated in similar groups (called "lemon sessions"), where they literally refined them**selves**. In the 1950s, the U.S. achieved the American dream. The broad middle class (roughly 80% of the population) had more than enough money to live well. The idea of "self-improvement" (literally improving one's **self**) became possible and began to become popular.

The "personal growth movement" of the late 1960s and 1970s brought the possibility of deliberately improving one's **self** to this great American middle class (that's most of us). T-groups, encounter groups, and therapy groups became available to anyone interested and willing to risk the experience.

Support groups sprang out of the energy of the women's movement and its "consciousness-raising" groups for women who were liberating them**selves** in what they experienced as a male-dominated culture. From these sprang some remarkable men's groups, such as my own (see the Introduction). Divorced, single, and business people's groups soon followed. Liberation from traditional roles was now possible for everyone.

Self-help groups began as experimental offshoots of therapy groups and quasi-religious movements. Recovery, Inc. (outpatient aftercare for former mental patients) and Alcoholics Anonymous (ex-drinkers supporting each other's sobriety) are examples of some of the oldest self-help group organizations. As the success of small-group process in helping people help themselves has become more obvious, it has been used effectively by such tiny organizations as the Diabetes Foundation and by such vast international businesses as Weight Watchers, Inc.

It is becoming increasingly apparent to the mental health establishment that small support groups are a vital source of the supportive **community** feeling that so many people desperately need in this fast-moving age of alienation. Many of us under fifty have never known the feeling of a small town, the camaraderie around a potbellied stove, or even friends and neighbors we can know and trust.

Most of our parents and grandparents gathered and built friendships with others through their old-world ethnic ties and neighbors, their churches, their work, and their extended families. Changes in the way we live today have eliminated these as real, meaningful social contact points. Small support groups can fill this gap. And for many of us who are living very differently from the way our parents' traditional nuclear families did, the intimate networks seem the way to have a close family feeling, even though the real thing doesn't exist or is too far removed geographically to help us.

The focus of this book is the deliberate creation of a men's **support** and **self-help** community.

Of the two types of groups mentioned above, **support groups** gather with more of a consciousness-raising, personal growth, feel-good focus, while **self-help groups** gather to deal with a specific problem and have a coping-better-with-the-problem focus. Yet they tend to become much the same type of group because they will naturally proceed through a very similar process. People in support groups learn how to feel good together and often help each other cope better with day-to-day hassles. People in self-help groups rapidly begin coping better with their shared problems through each other's willing assistance and understanding, and they often discover the wonderful, good feeling of growing as a person. So from this point on, I am including the function of self-help groups in any mention of support groups.

Friends, community, and personal growth all sound wonderful, but "is it going to change the world?" you ask. Some medical people have been saying there are people in our society who are literally dying of loneliness. And why not—what is there to live for if not other people and love? TV? A new car? Am I saying, "Change or die"? Well, in a way, yes I am. People living in an alienated world without connection to other people tend to act in ways destructive to themselves and our planet. In their desperation to feel OK, too often they will abuse themselves or others. Scared people caught up in shame could kill us all (see Chapter 30). Those who continue to build nuclear bombs, cut down rain forests, and dump toxic wastes are examples. Those of us who stay ignorant or do nothing are passively supporting the way it is. Perhaps we humans do need to change to continue to live on our planet.

Being in a group is a move in the direction of positive change. The process of being with other people in a safe, supportive situation can actually change who we think we are. For some of us in the group our heads will shrink painlessly, metaphorically speaking. For others a home-base group provides the safety necessary to experiment with life situations to grow a stronger and healthier sense of self. In a committed group each man will get what he needs, when he needs it. And as we grow closer to the essence of who we are, we tend to take more responsibility for our neighbors and our planet.

So let's live, let's change the world. Take the opportunity to create a richer life with real live men who laugh and love, who cry and care, who will be there for you just as you will be there for them. With a little help from this book and a little help from your new men friends, I invite you to live.

Why we grow!

When involved in an ongoing men's support group we are constantly exploring **new ways of being,** which expands our limited view of ourselves, other people, and life in general.

COMMITMENT

To create friendship, community, and intimacy

Without **commitment** the group doesn't work. Support groups are totally voluntary, and if the men don't come to "Group," it doesn't exist. Commitment ensures the longevity necessary to build the trust and safety essential to open up, risk, and share more of who we are.

Organizer's commitment

The first commitment is on the part of the organizer—you—to set a goal for the number of men you want in your group; then, using the next two chapters as a guide, take the steps necessary to bring your group together.

Time commitment

A basic agreement from **each** member of the group to stay with the group for a certain period of time is essential. Depending on the nature of the group, I recommend a minimum commitment of between six weeks and six months—six weeks for very specific skills-learning for problem-focused groups and six months for open-ended growth/support groups. Six weeks is just enough time to get to know everyone a bit and get a feel for what a group can be. Six months is time enough to get to know everyone fairly well. It usually takes one full year to get to know your group really well and two years splendidly.

Community commitment

Community is those people with whom we can truly be ourselves. If each member of your group has commitment to build community and friendship, it will help make the group a safe place.

In his wonderful 1987 book, *The Different Drum*, M. Scott Peck makes the distinction that "There is more than a quantum leap between an ordinary group and a community: they are entirely different phenomena." He provides a clear definition: "Community is a safe place precisely because no one is attempting to heal or convert you, to fix you, to change you. Instead, the members accept you as you are. You are free to be you. And being so free, you are free to discard defenses, masks, disguises: free to seek your own psychological and spiritual health."

Conflict commitment

My definition of conflict is simply: "You want one thing and I want another." So defined, conflict is a natural and important part of any relationship. The successful resolution of conflict will involve you and me telling the often hidden truth about why we want whatever it is we happen to want. In this open sharing we come to know new aspects of each other.

What is generally missing for us in our society is the safe space—the community—that supports our telling the truth at deeper levels. Your group is that opportunity. It is imperative that your group welcome conflict, and trust that you will know how to deal with it.

As M. Scott Peck says in *The Different Drum*: "The essential dynamic of pseudo-community is conflict-avoidance: true community is conflict-resolving."

It is through the successful resolution of conflict that we build intimacy.

Intimacy commitment

Intimacy is sharing those most private thoughts, feelings, and secret parts of ourselves over a long period of time. It is something we all need and crave—and few of us men have known the comfort or experienced the joy of true intimacy, especially with other men.

Intimacy and sexuality are terribly confused in our culture. Too many men seem painfully unaware of the great difference. Because we all want intimacy, we are vulnerable to advertising that uses women's sexuality to suggest that if we drink the right beer, drive the right car, or smoke the right cigarette, we will get this woman—and intimacy. After 10,000 repetitions we get the message that intimacy can be found only with beautiful women. This is a profound disservice to men.

"No, coach, it's not the money. He says your team lacks friendship, community, and intimacy."

The truth is that intimacy is possible with anyone willing. And intimacy rarely has anything to do with sexuality. Friendship, trust, and acceptance are what intimacy is about. And there is a connection between our ability to trust and accept ourselves and our true personal power.

Meeting the challenge of opening ourselves to others and finding acceptance is a vital step toward becoming able to know our own power. This is not the old dominating "power over," but the personal "power to"—to create our own lives as we want them to be. In the ability to be intimate is the power to trust and to love who you are at this moment. So relax, and make a commitment to intimacy.

To know greater intimacy
we often must take the risk of being hurt, laughed at, or rejected.
In the safety of your group, **committed** to emotionally supporting
each other and resolving conflict, you can afford to take those risks.
Your men's group will become a safe place, a refuge of comforting,
loving, and caring.

3

DECISIONS

What and who do I want in my group

The clearer you are on this chapter's title question, the greater your chances are of having a great group. Different men want different things, and a men's group can offer a wide range of new experiences and opportunities. Take the time to think about this and make honest choices about the group you want. Take out your pencil and check 'em off. (Note: You may want to photocopy these two pages, before you mark the boxes, to use with the men you will be interviewing.)

The purpose of my men's group is
Note: Choose one. Neither excludes the other, but picking one helps to focus your wants.
☐ Personal growth ☐ Shared fun, social activities

What I want from my men's group is
Note: You may check more than one and add your own.
☐ New friends ☐ Closer relationships with men
☐ Better communication skills ☐ Learn more about myself as a man
☐ Feeling of belonging ☐ Learn more about other men
☐ Become more relaxed in groups of men
☐ _____
☐ _____
☐ _____
☐ _____

Personal power qualities
Rate yourself first, then choose men like you.
Note: I recommend your group be close to how you rate yourself, because my experience is that men who are very shy simply do not mix well with men who are very assertive, either on a short-term or long-term basis.
☐ Aggressive ☐ Slightly held back
☐ Assertive ☐ Reserved
☐ Outgoing ☐ Shy

Present personal affiliations
Note: You may wish to include friends you already have. This will provide an initial sense of security and make the organizing easier. Or you may want to build a totally new cadre of friends from "strangers" (i.e., "friends not yet met").
☐ Friends ☐ Strangers
☐ Acquaintances ☐ Combination

The age of participants in my men's group is
   Rule of thumb: The most successful men's groups tend to have members who are fairly close in age. But the older men are, the less it seems to matter.

☐ 5 to 10 years older   ☐ 5 to 10 years younger
☐ 5 years either side of my age   ☐ Many ages combined
☐ Other _____

The number of men I want in my group is
   Note: I suggest that nine (9) is the ideal number of men for a support group. This is small enough to function when everyone is there and big enough to be a group if one, two, or even three are absent.

☐ 5   bare minimum
☐ 6 or 7   small, but workable
☐ 8 to 10   optimum
☐ 11 or 12   big, but workable
☐ 13   too big

Geographic considerations

☐ Local neighborhood—within walking distance
☐ Community—bicycle distance
☐ Citywide—within driving distance

When I want my group to meet is

	Mon.	Tue.	Wed.	Thu.	Fri.	Sat.	Sun.
Morning	☐	☐	☐	☐	☐	☐	☐
Afternoon	☐	☐	☐	☐	☐	☐	☐
Evening	☐	☐	☐	☐	☐	☐	☐

How often I want my group to meet is

☐ weekly   ☐ biweekly   ☐ monthly

How long I want my group meetings to be is

☐ 2 hours   ☐ 3 hours   ☐ 4 hours

   Now that you have decided the **Who's, Where's,** and **When's** for yourself, you can get on with the actual organizing of your group. If, as you talk with a prospective member of your group, you decide he seems appropriate, and if he is interested, you will be able to discuss with him the same choices you made on the above lists. If he is close enough to your choices, you will likely have a new group member.

   Now, as to actually finding the men to invite into your group, please go to Chapter 4.

ORGANIZING YOUR GROUP

How and where to find potential members

Other organizer

Note: If your group is already organized through your fraternal organization, school, church, or social service agency, you may skip this section and go on to Chapter 6 and begin planning your first meeting.

You as organizer

If you are organizing your own group, first let me encourage you. Aaron Kipnis says in his excellent new book, *Knights Without Armor*, "The myth of the lone hero is dead. As soon as a few men in a community raise the flag of male solidarity, healing, and fraternity, there's usually a rush to rally round. Many men are just waiting to come in from the cold. All it takes is one person to say, 'There's a men's meeting tonight.'" So, let me suggest some ways to find and choose the most appropriate men to make your group work well.

It will be easier and more familiar for you to use existing social structures, such as your church or synagogue, health or sports club, or perhaps your child's day-care center or school. Any connection through which you already have something in common may be a useful starting point.

If, however, such structures are not part of your life or you choose not to build your group through them, some of the following may be useful.

Finding appropriate men

Friends: If you have decided to include present friends in your group, I suggest you directly ask a friend or two to help organize. For example, ask each man to get two other men involved, or invite four other men to join and bring in one additional man each. This will provide a stable base for your group and will speed up the organizing process.

No friends: If you know what kind of group you want and have few or no men in mind (which, unfortunately, is common for men today; many of us never make another good friend after school or the military service), you may want to seek out local men from your immediate neighborhood, or extend your search citywide.

A lot can be accomplished with notices on bulletin boards in grocery stores, churches, and laundromats or by placing small ads in a community or alternative newspaper.

Examples of such personal notices and ads are presented on the following pages.

Local men's group example

> I am organizing a **Men's Support Group** for the purpose of building a new circle of
> friends, growing as a man by learning about myself through other men.
> I intend to have a good time in this unique social experience.
> I'm looking for men ages 25 to 35.
> If you want to be considered for this group, please contact me.
> Jeff Thomas (377-1852)

You may want to extend your group through a citywide search. A want ad
in the personal section of your newspaper will likely get you some results.

Citywide men's group examples

> Wanted: Men interested in a men's support group for new friendships; how to
> relate better to women (especially strong women); personal growth; and to get to
> know the "wildman within" … call Tom at 963-9887

or

> Men's Group: I am organizing a men's consciousness-raising group.
> Purpose: To explore male roles in society and learn to be more loving and less macho.
> Looking for married or single men between ages of 30 and 45.
> John 271-8932

Specialized men's groups

These notices can be more specific, because you are looking for a very select,
highly focused group of men, either by profession or situation.

Mutual interest specific groups: Men interested in mythology and ritual,
men married to powerful women, Vietnam veterans, men single too long, homo-
sexual/gay men, etc.

Example

> I've become intrigued by Joseph Campbell's work with mythology, especially the
> "rite of passage" rituals for men.
> I want to meet with other men for discussion and to learn from each other
> about male myths.
> If you would like to share this adventure, call Howard at 772-4381

Professionally specific groups: Teachers, computer operators, lawyers, social workers, accountants, salesmen, etc.

Examples

> Professional men wanted to join me in a support group for men.
> My purpose is to explore issues of men and power,
> also to provide mutual support and friendship ... Bob Purdy 572-9178

or

> Non-adversarial lawyers (sounds like an oxymoron), I know there are more like
> me out there, and I want us to support each other in this time of transition.
> We can learn from each other a way of feeling that works better than the thinking
> we were trained to do. Michael 829-7005

A few cautions

1. Some of the more provincial newspapers may refuse to carry a notice of the nature I've suggested. They are likely acting as public guardians, so all you can do is be honest about your intention and be willing to accept their answer.
2. Depending on what city you live in, it may be important to specify whether homosexual/gay men are to be included or not, to avoid any confusion. This can usually be done by including the word "straight" or "gay" in your notice.
3. Men may be skeptical and unsure. Though support groups have been a common phenomenon for over a decade, the idea is new to many men. They may need an explanation of the exact purpose. Be prepared.

Once men respond to your notice, you will need to discuss with them what you have in mind, and this may take the form of an interview. Go on to the next chapter.

"Instead of our usual Monday meeting, I think I'll just drum for a while. Feel free to join in on the chorus."

THE INTERVIEW

Who and how to choose group members

Choosing appropriate men to be part of your group is probably the single most important factor in creating a successful and enjoyable group. Making the right choice is often walking a fine line between being overcautious and too inclusive.

Some rule-of-thumb suggestions
1. Pick men similar to yourself in age, education, and social and economic background.
2. Pick men you **feel** good being with. (Trust your intuition here.)
3. Pick men truly interested. (Chapter 2 on Commitment)
4. Pick men with goals close to your own. (Chapter 3 on Decisions)

Doing an interview with a potential member of your group

I suggest you and/or your co-organizers arrange a time to get together with each man personally to get to know each other. This helps avoid surprises and gives you clearer information with which to make your decisions. The word "interview," if taken apart, literally means "you view me and I view you." It is an opportunity for men to "see" each other on several levels (physically, psychologically, philosophically) and make decisions about continuing a relationship.

Interview topics
There are some specific areas that I suggest be covered in your interviews.
1. What a **"support group"** is and how it works. Share this book with him, so he can see it has been done many times before.
2. **"Men's work"**! He may not yet know the value of men doing this type of mutual learning. Suggest he read *Knights Without Armor* by Aaron R. Kipnis, Ph.D., and/or *Fire in the Belly* by Sam Keen, or view the "A Gathering of Men" videotape of Bill Moyers interviewing Robert Bly. (Chapter 33, Recommended Books and Tapes)
3. **Leadership.** Explain that you are proposing an experiment and emphasize that through shared leadership **we** can create an excellent growth and caring experience.
4. **Intention!** Why does he want this group?
5. **Commitment!** Is he willing to **be there**?

Decision maker
Let each man interviewed know clearly and up front that it will be you and/or your co-organizers who decide on the membership of the group. You will

save later unnecessary stress if you can give each man some idea of your response during the process of the interview. For example: "It seems to me that we will work out okay, I'll let you know in two weeks," or "I'm sorry, it doesn't seem that we will work out for this experiment." Explain further if necessary, as graciously as possible.

Choosing the men
Specific qualities to look for in a potential good group member

1. Generally willing to take responsibility for his own thoughts, feelings, and actions
2. Reasonably in touch with his emotions (fear, joy, sadness, and anger)
3. Has concern about other people
4. Possesses fairly good verbal abilities
5. Willing and able to tolerate and handle some conflict
6. Capable of staying in the here and now (present time)

Characteristics to be wary of
Some cautions as to who not to invite into your group

1. **Manic**   hyperexcitable, can dominate the group out of deep-felt neediness
2. **Spacey**   disconnected thoughts may indicate serious internal conflict
3. **Very depressed** indicates serious underlying emotional problems and ought to seek a good therapist
4. **Men in crisis**   e.g., newly divorced, fired, etc. Check 'em out! The pain they are in can dominate and drag the group down. Better to see a counselor to work through the crisis and/or have time to let it pass (exception here is a self-help group where everyone shares the crisis. Example: divorce, or death of wife or child)
5. **Addicted**   currently addicted to alcohol or other drugs
6. **Isolated**   obvious fear of being emotionally/psychologically intimate
7. **Paranoid**   thinks he/she is being watched, copied, talked about, etc.

Some thoughts about numbers 4, 5, and 6 above

The reason many of us men need and enjoy a supportive men's group is because we have been terribly emotionally isolated, causing various crises in our lives. Too often we turn to "addictions." So take care not to rely too rigidly on the above cautions. If a man is **aware** of his situation and has the insight to appreciate the potential of the group, he may be on the road to fulfilling his personal needs and could become a good friend of yours. On the other hand, trust your gut feeling and say no if it feels right.

Another option: group interview

You might want to invite a group of prospective men together to get to know each other and discuss the possibility of a men's support group. This serves the additional function of giving them an actual experience of being in a men's group for at least that evening. You can cover the same five interview topics as the focus of your discussion. Or you might show the videotape "A Gathering of Men" as a powerful educational experience about men's work and how it has been rapidly evolving in our culture today.

The major downside of the group interview is that you have less control over making the final cuts. The group will tend to bond very quickly and it may be harder to let a man, who in a sense has already become part of the group, know he is no longer welcome. You may be inviting men you already know or have adequately interviewed over the phone, in which case you will no longer feel a need to control who gets to be a group member.

If you do not know the men invited to the group meeting interview, make it very clear up front, before the meeting begins, that you as organizer reserve the right to make that decision, and by when you will let them know. This is particularly important if some of the men are coming from a 12-step recovery community, because they are used to open and unlimited groups.

The group interview can be great fun and can generate huge and immediate support. So even if your group has only three men, they will quickly enjoy the feeling and will support the expansion of "their" new group. Build it, they will come!

*"We're going to bucket out **what**?! I thought we were going fishing!"*

"The new knights [Aaron Kipnis's own men's group] don't have any special chemistry or magic. We're not particularly brave, smart, cool, or lucky. We're essentially ordinary men who took the risk of reaching out to one another. We asked each other for help and offered it in return. We didn't pay anyone to be our expert healer. We just took turns. Fools and wise men all, stumbling along through the dark, being steadfast companions to one another in quest of masculine soul."
—Aaron R. Kipnis, Ph.D., *Knights Without Armor*

PART TWO
RUNNING YOUR MEN'S SUPPORT GROUP

"Nothing is more distinctive of the Old Being than the separation of man from man. Nothing is more passionately demanded than social healing. This is our ultimate concern and should be the infinite passion of every human being in every age."

—Paul Tillich

Preparation for the first meeting

Contact new members

You, as organizer, now have the pleasant task of contacting the men you have selected for your group. And it is your challenging task to complete the communication with men who have not been selected, if you were not able to make that decision at the time of the interview. Chances are they will appreciate your integrity and courage in calling and will forgive you for having made a decision not in their favor.

On the following page is a form letter that you can adapt, or photocopy, and use to contact the men invited into your group. Feel free to rewrite it and change it in any way that suits your needs. A phone call to verify that each man got the letter will reestablish personal contact, demonstrate your interest, and make it easier for them to show up. You could also do it by phone and forget about the letter. Share the phone calling with your co-organizer.

Group leader

At this point in the process of bringing the group together, you are the central focus because you are the only man whom everyone has met. You are the group leader. While this is unavoidable now, you will be working toward making the group a democratic collective of men who take on and own fully the responsibility for "their" group.

To prepare, read and understand the information in Chapter 7 before your new group gathers together. Then follow the steps! If you feel too uncertain, get help and leadership support (choose a co-leader) for the first meeting or two. It might also be more fun.

For the first three meetings, you (and/or your co-leader) will be leading fully. With the beginning of the fourth meeting you begin sharing leadership, and continue to do so until your group develops the procedure that works best for you.

Where to meet

There are many possibilities. The man with the biggest living room and the fewest family members roaming around might be the most appropriate host. A more neutral spot might be a school, church, club, or private restaurant room. Establishing a consistent place for the first few months has a valuable stabilizing effect. After that, a round-robin process of going alternately to each man's home affords everyone the opportunity to get to know each other's lifestyle better, and lets every man experience the host jitters periodically. Usually a group will then settle into one place for a while. One man I know turned his unused basement family room into a *kiva* with Native American art and animal carvings. There his group can feel safe drumming and meeting very privately.

Length of meeting time

I recommend three hours each week or every other week. Consult with your group as to what will work best. Or experiment for a month one way, then try another.

Welcome letter

Dear ———————————— ,

Welcome to **your** men's group! Our group will be your opportunity to create some new friendships, develop and practice new skills, and generally get to know more about who we are as men to improve the quality of our lives.

How are we going to do this? Step by step, week by week, we will be having a great time learning self-awareness skills, communication skills, and group leadership skills. With these as a base, over the months we will be able to get to know, trust, and be with each other as men in a remarkable new way.

Our first meeting will be:

———————————————— from —————— until ——————
       (date)   (time)

————————————————————————————————
(address with specific streets and landmarks, if necessary)

If you have any questions, phone me at ————————————————
Looking forward to seeing you,

(signed)

THE FIRST MEETING

Getting to know ya

Excited about the first meeting

Having read and taken the organizing steps of the preceding chapters, you have come to the crucial next step in the life of your men's group: the first meeting. It is natural to feel scared, excited, nervous, and many other emotions. This is a good sign! These emotions suggest that this group is important to you. Read and understand the following information before your new group gathers together, then follow the steps. If you feel too uncertain, get help from a co-leader for the first couple of meetings.

The first meeting will probably be a time of high excitement, apprehension, and uncertainty for all the new group members. This is one reason I have designed an agenda. The other reason is you. From years of experience with new group leaders, I know they usually need something to hang onto.

What I have put together is a complete word-for-word walk-through of the process of leading the first several sessions. This will give you whatever level of structure you need to make your group go. If you have never led any kind of group and need to read word for word—do it! If you have some experience and trust yourself enough to wing it with your own words—do it! The bottom line is doing what works to guide these men into becoming a reasonably skilled self-led group.

I have included lots of material and activities to be covered **step by step**. The steps of the process are set up to build trust in the group as quickly as possible. **Trust the process**. The number of structured steps will decrease as weeks go by and your group becomes closer and more stable.

Read this chapter a couple of times and prepare in advance. Men who do not have their own book will need the two handouts on pages 24 through 26. Make enough copies for everyone.

GROUP STEP 1

Name tags: It's important for the men to feel comfortable in this new "support" group. Name tags simply help to make first contacts. Give them out as men arrive at the meeting place.

Starting time: Begin when everyone gets there. Or, if everyone is not there by starting time, wait **ten minutes**, and if all are not there by then, ask the group if it wants to start. If so, begin.

Introduction round: Usually if each man says something in turn, everyone relaxes. So, your first action is to invite everyone to say his name, how he found out about the group, and his reasons for coming. This will break the ice and get some information out for men to share. As the men share information and recognize similar reasons for participating, they will feel more comfortable and committed to the group. Here we go.

Leader Action 1

Informally welcome everyone, and begin by inviting brief self-introductions. (The material in italics are suggested word-for-word scripts you might use. Feel free to adapt them into your own words.) Say: *"Let's get started. Please say your name, how you found out about this group, and what is one thing you would like to get from this group. I'll start, then we'll go around to the right."* You have just established the first ritual in your new group. We will come to call it "rounds." If you have already chosen to use another opening ritual (perhaps from Chapter 26), introduce it now.

GROUP STEP 2

Goals: It is important to get individual and group goals clear. Clarifying our wants reinforces them in our bodies and minds. This is another way of saying that we create our own reality. For this reason I have included written goals right at the beginning. I suggest that each man become aware of his immediate goals and intentions for himself in his group. You will ask the men to write out their immediate, intermediate, and long-term goals. You might invite the men to be aware of their feelings and bodies (they are really the same) and focus their consciousness on exactly what each intends to get from this group.

Leader Action 2

Ask the men to open their books to "Goals" (page 24, or hand out photocopies). Each man fills in his own goals and wants for this group, for the next six weeks, six months, and for the long term. Say: *"This is yours to use. Please take your time, be thoughtful, feel relaxed, and complete this page. It's important. If you feel stuck, take a deep breath and write the next goal that comes to mind. Please continue until you feel complete with your goals list."* Take about eight to ten minutes for this activity.

GROUP STEP 3

(Skills training #1)

It is now time for the men in your group to get to know each other a little better and learn a valuable communication skill in the process.

Leader Action 3

Statements and "I" statements: instructional sequence

1. Be sure the group understands the purpose of this experiment. Say: *"This activity is a way to break the ice and begin giving everyone an opportunity to get to know individual men better. It also teaches a useful commu-*

nication skill. It is easy. I will walk you through a series of communication experiences, stopping every so often to talk about what we learned. Are you ready?"

2. Have everyone in the group choose a partner or new friend (preferably a man they don't know, because this normally makes it easier to risk experimenting with new behavior). Say: *"Pick a partner, preferably a man you don't know. Once you have your partner, find a place to sit separate from others."*

3. Ask each man to begin to get to know his new partner using no questions, only statements. Do this just as written. It's fun. Say: *"Now, imagine you are at a party and you just met this guy and you begin a normal conversation, with only one picky little difference: no questions, no questions at all. Okay, any questions?"* Wait half a second and then quickly say: *"Very good, begin."*

4. Stop the process after three to five minutes. Say: *"Stop."*

5. Invite feedback to the group on what the experience was like for individuals. Say slowly: *"I wonder how that felt to you. I'm curious as to what it was like for you to get to know someone new without questions. I want to know what was different or what you learned."*
   Give this seven to ten minutes, or until energy wanes.

6. Go on to the second part. Ask the men to continue their conversation without questions and to make each statement an "I" statement. *"This time again, only statements, but use 'I' as the first word or within every sentence to speak totally about yourself."* It helps to model this skill for a new group by emphasizing the "I." Say: *"**I** want you to begin."*

7. Stop process after three to five minutes. Say: *"**I** want you to stop."*

8. Ask for feedback to the group (not to you; this is mutual learning). *"I wonder what **your** experience was in that exercise. I want you to share with the whole group what happened for **you**."* Be aware of responses, and assist men in changing any "you" statements into "I" statements. *"Speak for yourself, make 'I' statements."*

9. To clarify understanding, discuss with the group the usefulness of this skill within and outside the group. Begin with: *"When men use 'I' statements they are owning their thoughts, feelings, and actions, which is what we want in this group."*

10. Suggest an agreement within the group that everyone use this skill and

help each other in learning it. Say: *"I suggest that we agree to support each other in making 'I' statements."*

11. Move on to the "introduction of partner" process. Say: *"Let's all get back together now and briefly introduce our new friend to the group."*

12. Optional discussion process: Say: *"The author of* A Circle of Men *says that the use of 'I' statements is the single most valuable self-awareness communication skill. Using this simple skill will change most men's consciousness significantly. What do you think he means?"* Discuss.

Note: Because he is an equal group member it is very important that the leader choose a partner himself and participate in this and all other activities. If there is an uneven number of men, have one three-man group.

Take a break: Ten to fifteen minutes, enjoy some refreshments, hang out, and chat.

GROUP STEP 4

The next step is to discuss rules, agreements, and guidelines. On pages 25 and 26 I've provided a list of these that have worked well in the past. If you or your group want to change any of them, please do so. I suggest you keep them as simple as possible.

Leader Action 4

Call the group back together after the break. Invite them to open their books to page 25 and 26 or hand out copies of "Rules, Agreements, and Guidelines for Men's Groups."

Say: *"I would like to discuss these rules and agreements so that we all have an opportunity to say how we feel about them. After all, this is **our** group! Let's go through them one at a time and see if we have agreement on all of these?"* Ten to fifteen minutes should be enough time. If the group gets stuck on an item, put it on the agenda for another time.

Move to the ten "Guidelines." They will greatly help the group to progress well over the weeks and months to come. They provide a common reference point for group procedure. Begin the discussion by saying:

*"Okay, let's move on to the guidelines and get an understanding of them. They seem to be a useful set of ideas, though probably open to some interpretation. We will spend some special time working on the guideline about confidentiality because it is **our** group."*

Continue the discussion until you get to number 10 on confidentiality.

Say: *"Just what does this mean about confidentiality, what are we agreeing to, how much can be shared outside this group?"*

Continue the discussion until some consensus has been reached, restate it, and if everyone agrees, write it down.

GROUP STEP 5

Discussion: Depending on the time, either move on to the closing activity, or if you have more time, open a discussion about goals for **"our"** group, from earlier written goals.

Leader Action 5

Say: *"Let's focus on sharing our goals for this group, from what we wrote earlier. It will be a way of getting to know each other and our expectations."*

GROUP STEP 6

Closing the group: Every group requires a definite beginning and ending. Just as we started with rounds, we will close with rounds. Sometimes we call closing rounds The Whip Round because it is usually shorter. As your group progresses over the weeks, put more emphasis on the disclosure of feelings, not just general comments such as: "I'm okay," or "I'm all right." As the group moves through the steps, these activities will become more spontaneous and less structured.

Leader Action 6

About ten minutes before the agreed ending time, say: *"It is time to end our meeting. Next week we will continue with some more skills training. Now, let's close this group meeting by doing another quick go-around the group. Let's all say how we are feeling now, what was our experience at this meeting, and what is our commitment. I'll be glad to start, because you will all get opportunities to be the leader soon. . . ."*

GROUP STEP 7

Introduce and do whatever closing ritual you may have chosen (see Chapters 25 and 26) and say good-bye.

". . . then after he quit his job, he came home, burned down the garage, and built a sweat lodge . . ."

Name: _____ Date: _____

Men's group goals form

Goals: What you want is what you get: Your wants for your new men's group might include friendship, personal growth, support, the sharing of activities, a change in your life, contacts, learning social skills, etc. It is important to **write** what **you** want! Be specific!

My goals for the first six weeks in my group are:

1. _____
2. _____
3. _____
4. _____
5. _____

My goals for the first six months in my group are:

1. _____
2. _____
3. _____

My long-range (one to three years) goals in my group are:

1. _____
2. _____

A Credo:
Taking full responsibility to risk being real!

In our men's group we each take responsibility for ourselves.
To the greatest of our ability we respond to our own needs
and wants at every moment and trust that in doing so we will serve
each other's greatest good.
As I take increasing responsibility for myself I become a more real,
authentic, and credible man for you to interact with.
If I give you feedback I will take responsibility to tell you graciously
about anything I experience that is in conflict with my needs or wants,
trusting that we will enter into dialogue with open minds.

 A Circle of Men: The Original Manual for Men's Support Groups © 1992 Bill Kauth

Rules, agreements, and guidelines for men's groups

Rules: Non-negotiable items essential to the growth and survival of the group.

1. **Take full responsibility for yourself.** This is **your** group, and **you** are responsible for getting what **you** want.
2. **Tell the truth.** To the best of your ability, let others know what is happening for you.

Agreements: Items that you all agree with. These will make any group work better.

1. **If you are going to be late or absent, call someone.** This saves waiting and wondering.
2. **Don't leave the group permanently without saying "good-bye."** An unannounced dropout is like a death in the family and can result in much confusion for other group members.
3. **No drug use before group.** Drug use (including alcohol, of course) can cause different states of consciousness in the group, often creating confusion and an unproductive, unsatisfying meeting.
4. **Lite drug use during group.** Use of caffeine, nicotine, and sugar can alter consciousness and/or be distracting and annoying to group members. Make some agreements.

 A Circle of Men: The Original Manual for Men's Support Groups © 1992 Bill Kauth

Guidelines: The purpose of these ground rules is to enhance **contact** among members and to encourage each man to **take responsibility** for the thoughts, feelings, or statements he directs to the group at large or to one other man.

1. **Speak freely and openly.** Men need not ask permission to speak, intervene, move around, or contribute in any fashion. However, it is easier if only one man speaks at a time.

2. **Speak directly to another man.** Instead of "Bob seems sad," speak to him: "Bob, you seem sad to me," or "I imagine you are angry right now."

3. **Any man may "pass."** If someone is uncomfortable with a learning experience or topic, he has the right not to participate.

4. **Be aware of feelings.** Express them. Because avoidance of feelings is so ingrained, give special attention to how men feel, and encourage feeling statements. "I feel happy" or "I'm afraid."

5. **Be here now.** Emphasize the present. As much as possible, stay in the here and now by describing present-time experience.

6. **Use "I" statements.** Rather than using the editorial "we" or "you," speak for yourself. "I feel comfortable."

7. **Avoid questions, especially "why" questions.** Before asking a question (or answering one) consider the statement behind your question and express the direct statement instead. Example:

    Question: "Why are you looking at me?"

    Statement: "I'm not comfortable when you look at me like that."

8. **Say "man" or "men."** Taking back a healthy identity as men requires clear language. Stay away from "people" or "person" when referring to each other. This is a **men's** group.

9. **Avoid judgments; be descriptive.** Describe the man's behavior and your response. In this way you do not lay a trip on someone else, and you take responsibility for your own reactions. Example:

    Instead of: "You're really off base."

    You might say: "When you ramble on, I lose a sense of where you are going, and I start to feel anxious."

10. **Confidentiality.** To increase the sense of safety within the group, it works well to establish some consensus agreement as to what is and what is not "confidential." Discuss it!

THE SECOND MEETING

Great to see ya again

This meeting is not only crucial to the life of the group, but it may be important to you in a very personal way. At the second meeting you discover who has decided to come back. This is a big step for group members to make in terms of commitment to the group. You may feel rejected if some men do not come back. However, I invite you to keep in mind that it is usually their discomfort with the group situation, rather than with an individual, that has caused them to drop out. That's why I suggest taking in at the beginning a few more men than the optimum number for your group. If group members would like to discuss this situation, do so.

The second meeting is going to focus on some very useful group learning experiences as part of your discussion. These experiences include: the ritual for **opening your meeting** and skills for **heightening personal awareness**. Together, these learning experiences will increase ownership, spontaneity, and organization within your group.

GROUP STEP 1

Rounds is the very first group activity of your meetings. Rounds serves a number of valuable purposes.

> First, it quickly becomes an **opening ritual** that is consistent and signals the official beginning of the group meeting. This is important, because new groups need structure.
> Second, Rounds creates an **agenda** into which all members have input and it establishes some of the **focus** for the meeting.
> Finally, Rounds is a way for men to start talking in the group and **making contact** with each other.

I believe this is so important that I have included a **Rounds** handout at the end of this chapter, to be duplicated and given to all members who do not have this book.

Timing: Rounds can very easily dominate the entire length of the meeting, so it works best to limit each man's rounds "check-in" to a maximum of five minutes. Let this be known right away, as I have noted in "Leader Action 1." If a man needs more time to discuss something or get feedback, he asks for it in step 3.

Rotating leadership: Before we move on to the leader action, I want to mention one more thing. It is important that by the fourth group meeting someone besides the original leader begins Rounds. The original leader is only to get the group started! After that, it is important that all members get opportunities to open and direct the group.

Leader Action 1 ━━━━━━━━━━━━━━━━━━━━━━━━━━━━━━━

Hand out to all members copies of the handout entitled "Rounds."

Say: *"I would like to begin the group with Rounds, which is explained in the handout that you all have. This is an easy way to begin our meetings and will help us talk together. Especially for this second meeting, it's a good way to reintroduce ourselves and welcome each other back. Rounds will always consist of your sharing present feelings, news in your life since the last meeting, and what you want from this meeting—and an optional wild card. Rounds needs to be kept to under five minutes per man.*

"Because I'm the leader this week, I get to pick the wild card. It will be: What was the best thing that happened to you this last week? I'll be glad to start. My name is . . . I'm feeling . . . I want from this meeting . . . The best thing was . . ." (Time: ten to thirty minutes, depending on the size of the group)

After Rounds has gone **around** the circle, the leader briefly summarizes the energy and wants of the group. Any special concerns and the agenda are mentioned. Do not take more than one minute for this summation. An example might go something like this:

"It seems that most of us are feeling pretty good tonight and had some good things happen during the week. It also seems that a couple of us could use a little fire-up energy, especially you, John, because you asked for specific encouragement.

"Our objectives seem to include getting to know each other better tonight, discussing our fear of women's criticism, and hearing about the specific issues that Joe and Edward brought up. Would anyone care to add something I missed?"

(Time: Thirty seconds to one minute)

GROUP STEP 2 ━━━━━━━━━━━━━━━━━━━━━━━━━━━━━━━━━━━

Awareness: The next step in our group is to discuss awareness and do an awareness learning experience. Increased awareness of self and others is a fundamental learning experience; for many men, it is a significant reason for joining a group such as this. To set the stage, hand out copies of the last page of this chapter. This activity and discussion will help the group become closer and be more aware of what is going on between members.

Leader Action 2 ━━━━━━━━━━━━━━━━━━━━━━━━━━━━━━━

After all members have looked at the awareness page, say:

"All change begins with awareness, so our level of awareness will deter-

mine what happens in the group. I want to begin our learning about awareness with someone reading the Dan Millman quotes about awareness. Who would be willing to read them out loud?"

After quotes are read, ask for discussion.

When the discussion is complete, say:

"Awareness of awareness is a neat trick. Perhaps it can be further explained by something called the awareness spectrum. Full awareness is a combination of various body, mind, and spirit parts of us. Using the spectrum we can examine the parts of the whole."

As members ask questions and make comments, there will probably be some confusion. Then say:

"To help us all understand the process better, I want to move on to the awareness activity. It is an opportunity to explore the areas of the awareness spectrum. I'll take you through the activities step by step."

Do the activities, taking care to discuss the results after each step.

Self and other awareness: instructional sequence, step by step

1. *"Pick a partner, if possible a man you don't know yet.*
2. *Sit directly opposite your new partner so you can see him.*
3. *We will start with sensation/physical data function. Notice your partner. What do you see? SEE!*
4. *Tell your partner what you see. (Examples: 'I'm aware of your blue shirt, I'm aware of your brown hair, I'm aware of your mustache.') Be totally objective. Do not use subjective adjectives like 'good-looking,' 'strange,' or 'interesting.' Alternate statements back and forth* (take turns). *Tell your partner what you see and only what you see."*

   Two minutes and stop.
5. *"Give feedback to the group. What was your experience in this exercise, how did you feel?"*

   Stay with feedback until energy fades, then move to the next part.
6. *"Now look at your partner again, and this time see the more subtle body language. Be aware and report what you see. No interpretations. (Example: 'I'm aware that your legs are crossed, I'm aware that your eyebrow is raised.')"*

   Alternate back and forth.
7. Stop process after two minutes. Ask for feedback from group. *"What was your experience? Was it different this time?"*

   Two to five minutes and move on.
8. We are now going to make the leap into the intuitive/knowing function. Say: *"Now, without thinking about it, tell your partner what you are feeling about him, any sense you have of his feelings or energy right now."*

   Two minutes, then ask for discussion.
9. Next we will move into the interpreting/thinking function. *"I want you alternately to share with your partner what you see and what you think it*

means. (Examples: 'I see that you are wearing jeans and I think you are a casual guy,' or 'I hear your soft voice, and I think you are a gentle sort of man.' Or: 'I see you looking directly at me and I think you are a powerful man.') Use 'I see/hear and I think.' "

Two or three minutes, and stop.

10. *"Now quietly be aware of your partner with no interpretations. Just see him without any opinion. Feel him."* Pause one minute. *"Just be there with another loving man, with no words getting in the way."*

Three minutes.

11. Take feedback. *"What was your experience, what did you notice? How did you feel about the interpretations and with no interpretations? Discuss the value of both parts of this process to full and open communication."* These skills will be useful to each other through giving our honest feedback later on.

12. *"Now for the last part, become aware of yourself and report to your partner—in the same format we just used—your awareness of yourself and what you think it means. (Example: 'I'm aware that my stomach is tight, and I think I am hungry. I'm aware of wiggling my foot, and I think this exercise makes me nervous.') Alternate as before."* Stop after two or three minutes. *"Now quietly be aware of yourself with no interpretations. Just feel you, without any opinion."*

13. Stop after two or three minutes and take feedback. *"Give feedback to the group. How did you feel reporting self-awareness interpretations, and then just being aware with no interpretations? What was different?"*

14. Unstructured conversation between partners: *"Share how this exercise was for you and straighten out any misinterpretations about each other as you continue getting to know your partner."*

Five minutes and stop.

15. Group discussion: *"Let's discuss as a full group how awareness can enhance the feeling of closeness. And how did it feel to cross normal boundaries with another man and ourselves? Is it possible to feel 'intimacy'?"*

Ten minutes or until energy fades.

Break time: Take time for hang'n' out, drink some water, munch some snacks.

GROUP STEP 3

Group discussion: Depending on the length of time your group meets, you may be ready to end or may have some time remaining to do optional stuff. If there is time available I suggest the following:

For groups that have gotten together to discuss very specific issues, it is important that a discussion take place, because it is the members' more immediate need. For groups that have no specific agenda or needs, I suggest that you use the "wants" that members brought up during Rounds as a focus for discussion. Or work with individual issues men brought up in Rounds.

Leader Action 3

Move the group into a discussion or issues from earlier in the meeting.
Say: *"Let's use some of our new awareness skills to discuss (or work with) some of the issues brought up earlier in the meeting."*

GROUP STEP 4

Closing the group: After a satisfactory discussion has taken place or it is time to end the meeting, a closing activity is needed. Closing Rounds, or **The Whip Round**, is this activity. It is a quick opportunity that provides closure and promotes self-responsibility.

Leader Action 4

Introduce The Whip Round.
Say: *"I want to end the group tonight (or today) with The Whip Round, which is a kind of closing Rounds. Let's go around the circle and each man say how you are feeling now and if you got what you wanted, if you have any 'unfinished business' before we end, and maybe what you want for next week. Quickly now, who wants to start?"*
When everyone has finished, move to your closing ritual.

GROUP STEP 5

Reintroduce and do whatever closing ritual you may have chosen and say good-bye.

"Okay, you've brought me here, Cowboy Bob, but I'm still not thirsty."

Rounds:

a group

opening

technique

and ritual

Contents of Rounds	Purpose
1. How I'm feeling right now	to be in present time
2. Report on the week past	to establish continuity
3. What I want for myself tonight	to set the agenda
4. *Wild Card* or themes (optional)	to share information and have fun
5. Summary of the group's energy and wants (by group leader)	to provide focus and direction

Suggestions for Wild Cards or Themes for Rounds (See #4 above)

1. What is the most positive thing that has happened to you over the past week?

2. When did you have the most fun or enjoyment during the week?

3. What is the most exciting positive thought or idea you have had during the past week?

4. Describe the most positive thing you did for another person this past week.

5. Tell something you like about yourself as a man.

6. Tell something you like about another man in this room.

7. Share one of the most scary (or sad, or joyous) times you have ever had in ming challenge in your life?

8. Where is your home town and how do you feel about it?

9. What is your birth order in your fasmily of origin?

10. What is the most significant upcoming challenge in your life?

11. What would be a perfect two-hour group meeting for you?

12. What color and sound corresponds with how you're feeling right now?

13. What life experience would you like to do with someone else—and alone?

14. What animal do you see yourself as?

15. Describe something you learned from a mistake.

16. Who are the three people who have influenced the most change in your life?

17. One thing I am embarrassed about is—and why.

18. My all-time favorite movie is—and as exactly as possible tell why.

19. If I could be any living person, I would be—(can also be a historical figure).

20. And so on. Be creative! What do you want to know about the men in your group?

A Circle of Men: The Original Manual for Men's Support Groups © 1992 Bill Kauth

Life is a great school, and nature is the ultimate teacher—but without **awareness**, you can't hear the "teacher." **Awareness** transforms life's lessons into wisdom; it can translate confusing circumstances and events into useful knowledge. **Awareness**, then, is the beginning of all learning.

If **awareness** is obstructed or weak, learning does not take place—or if it does take place, it is random and haphazard. Trying to learn a skill without total **awareness** is like trying to apply a stamp without adhesive—it just won't stick.

One sure sign of growing **awareness** is that you "feel" as if you are getting worse. **Awareness** is literally a disillusioning process, because it cuts through illusions; it entails a momentary drop in self-esteem, a dent in our self-image. No one likes to look at his weaknesses, so we all have a tendency to resist **awareness**.

True **awareness** is a sensitivity of the entire organism arrived at through sensory feedback, mental clarity, and emotional intuition. If it were merely an intellectual affair, then babies couldn't learn.

Warrior Athlete: Training Mind, Body, and Spirit, by Dan Millman. Stillpoint Publishing, Walpole, NH 03608 (Used by permission)

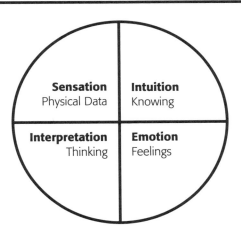

Selective awareness is consciousness focused on one function.

Sensation: We experience the world and other people around us through our physical senses of sight, sound, smell, touch, and taste.
Intuition: We know through what is often called our sixth sense. A "knowing" separate from our usual physical input.
Interpretation: We analyze the input and give meaning to what we perceive and remember from past experiences. Often called thinking or mental process.
Emotion: We have physical body responses often called feelings. Sad, mad, glad, and scared are the basic emotions.

Full or true awareness is the combination of all the functions.

THE THIRD MEETING

Feeling and thinking

Hello again. During this third meeting, we're going to be following up on the process of awareness we began at the last meeting. You might be wondering why I'm putting so much emphasis on the concept of awareness. As I mentioned in the last chapter, without awareness, nothing changes. Awareness is the basis for all meaningful human interaction. It is also the basis for all the activities in this book.

In our last meeting we looked at the awareness spectrum and worked with all the functions except emotion/feeling. This entire meeting focuses on the **emotion/feeling** function. It will be contrasted with the **interpreting/thinking** function because for men this distinction is imperative. There are significant differences between feeling and thinking. We men have been largely cut off from our feelings. We were raised to minimize our feelings and pay attention to logic. Thinking is often the only process we know, and the only way we know to give meaning to life. We've been led to believe that thinking is a superior function, to the point that many of us have become trapped in this very limited mode of being.

In this meeting we are focusing on feeling and thinking, because new awarenesses gained in these areas will have a radical effect on this group and your life. As you go through this meeting's activities, be sensitive to the differences between these two functions and their effects.

GROUP STEP 1

Just as in the last meeting we began with Rounds, so we will this time. As a matter of fact, we always will, because Rounds, as you now know, is an opening ritual that focuses members' attention on the group, makes men feel a sense of membership, and sets the agenda.

Leader Action 1

Review the handout from our last meeting entitled Rounds. Choose one of the wild card questions to ask and say:

"I want to welcome everyone back again and I'd like to start with our usual opening activity: Rounds. I've picked question number [choose one] from the Rounds handout we got last meeting. I would prefer not to start, so who wants to begin?"

By having someone else start, the group begins to distribute the leadership among participants other than the original leader.

GROUP STEP 2

The next step in our group is to discuss feeling and thinking. Then we'll do some clarification activities to become more clear on the distinction between feeling and thinking. This will also be an opportunity to get to know your co-members a little better.

Leader Action 2

1. Have all members sit comfortably in a circle with their eyes closed and their bodies relaxed. Have members take slow, deep breaths and consciously relax muscles. Then say: *"This activity is a way to gain greater awareness of the difference between thinking and feeling. With your eyes closed, I want you to focus your awareness outside of this room into the area outside this building. Listen for sounds or other sensations and try to name the cause of those sensations. Identify as many as possible."*

After about three minutes, have members open their eyes.

2. Have them immediately break into pairs and identify as many sources of the sensations as possible. To do this, say: *"Now I want you to choose a partner, pair up with a man you haven't been with before. The first step of this activity is to compare what we were aware of in the outside zone. Please discuss your awareness with your partner. Do you notice a distinction between your observations of thinking and feelings?"* (Five to seven minutes)

3. Now come back together into the full group. The original leader (or whoever has responsibility for this training segment) gives a brief talk on the distinction between thinking and feeling.

> "The male has paid a heavy price for his masculine 'privilege' and power. He is out of touch with his emotions and his body. Only a new way of perceiving himself can unlock him from old, destructive patterns and enrich his life."
>
> —Herb Goldberg,
> *The Hazards of Being Male*

Thinking and feeling: the distinction

Thinking is a cerebral process: thoughts, opinions, judgments, ideas, and external observations. Analyzing, calculating, and figuring stuff out. Example: How many men's names can you "think" of that start with "B"? What is the best way to get from New York to Los Angeles?

Feelings are awareness in the body, truth responses, and "gut" reactions. It is important to note that the word "feelings" is also used for touch sensations and intuitive hunches. Here we mean only the emotions. Examples of the four basic emotions and other words for them (also see "The Four Basic Emotions" handout):

Glad: happy, excited, delighted, warm
Sad: misty, heavy, guilty, lost
Mad: angry, irritated, annoyed, rageful
Scared: fearful, apprehensive, anxious, terrified

4. Invite everyone to participate in the following "thinking-feeling" rounds. Know that the learning is in the doing. Say: *"Let's do a thinking round. I want everyone to make a simple thinking statement. Who wants to begin?"* Continue around to the left. (Examples: I think it is too hot today, I think baseball is boring, I think this group is going to stick together for a long time.) Gently make an observation if someone states a feeling rather than a thought, then move on.

5. When the round is complete, say: *"Now let's do a feeling round. State either what you are feeling now or make up a feeling. Continue where we started and around to the left."* (Examples: I feel excited, I feel anxious, I feel terrific about being with this group.) Make brief observations/corrections if someone states a thought for a feeling: *"May I suggest that sounds like an opinion, which would make it a thought, so try another feeling. Good, thanks."* Move on quickly, don't get stuck in the process with anyone.

6. When complete, do another round of thoughts and another round of feelings. Invite group members to add briefly any observations or corrections they may have. Keep the round moving. When all four rounds are complete, ask for discussion of the distinction between thinking and feeling.

GROUP STEP 3

Group discussion: Once again, your group may be ready to end or may have time to do more. You may want to use topics from rounds as a discussion stimulus, or work with individual issues brought up in rounds.

Leader Action 3

Move the group into a discussion or personal work. Say: *"Let's use our new awareness of thinking and feeling to discuss (or work with) some of the issues brought up earlier in the meeting."*

GROUP STEP 4

Begin rotating the leadership: It is important that by the fourth group meeting (next time) another man besides the original leader begins rounds. The original leader is only to get the group started! Remember, the more responsibility you take, the less the group takes. This is why next week you do not lead rounds.

Leader Action 4

Say: *"It's time to pass on the group leadership tasks. We need a volunteer to do the opening and closing rounds for our next meeting. Who is ready?"* Take whoever volunteers and make sure he has a copy of this book or the Rounds handout. He may even be interested in co-leading the listening activity for the next meeting.

GROUP STEP 5

Closing the group: Invite everybody to share their present feelings with a whip round. Don't let men leave with **"unfinished business."** And finally, encourage your group to make physical contact, such as shaking hands or giving a hug, to get a feeling of individual completion with each other man. We men sometimes need a little support to say good-bye in a physical way.

My friend Jared suggested a powerful closing ritual his group uses. They link arms over shoulders in a close circle for as long as it takes for each man to make and hold eye contact with all of the other men in turn. It takes about a minute and a half. He says it's much scarier and more intimate, and ultimately more personal and bonding, than even hugging (which they go on to do individually as they break, anyway).

Leader Action 5

Say: *"So, it's time to end. Let's do a whip round. How are you feeling now? Is there any unfinished business, that is, anything that needs to be said to anyone in the group so it will not be carried until our next meeting? Say it now. And I want to suggest that we make some physical contact with each other as we say good-bye. Perhaps a handshake or a hug, whatever feels right to you."*

GROUP STEP 6

Reintroduce and do whatever closing ritual you may have chosen and say good-bye in a physical way. You as leader get to demonstrate it.

"We need to develop a calmness about masculine power so we don't have to act out dominating, disempowering behavior toward others."
—Robert Moore and Douglas Gillette, *King, Warrior, Magician, Lover*

The four basic emotions

◯ = Me ☐ = What I want

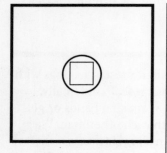 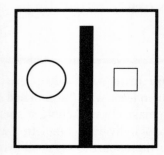 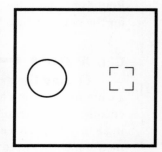 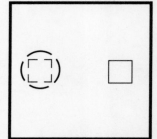

Glad	**Mad**	**Sad**	**Scared**
I have what I need/want.	Something is blocking the attainment of what I need/want.	I've lost something that I needed/wanted.	I may (unknown) lose myself and what I have, while trying to attain what I need/want.
Other words for and intensities of this emotion Loved, Appreciated, Satisfied, Happy, Excited, Peaceful, Enthused, Pleased, Tender, Accepted, Content, Joyous	**Other words for and intensities of this emotion** Angry, Hateful, Frustrated, Hurt, Hostile, Aggravated, Mean, Irritated, Annoyed, Worried, Enraged	**Other words for and intensities of this emotion** Helpless, Rejected, Grieved, Disappointed, Lonely, Deserted, Empty, Alone, Lost, Heavy	**Other words for and intensities of this emotion** Fearful, Anxious, Overwhelmed, Afraid, Nervous, Terrified, Insecure, Vulnerable, Weak
	What do I need/want? What is blocking?	**What have I lost?**	**What do I need/want to know?**
Action Enjoy the feeling!	**Action** Determine the need/want and what the block is. Express the feeling. Remove the block and satisfy the need/want.	**Action** Determine the loss. Acknowledge the loss. Grieve the loss.	**Action** Gather information. Act . . . "walk" through the fear . . . get to the other side . . . then look back.

Note: Shame is often considered an emotion. I think of it as an identity rooted in fear and grief.

A Circle of Men: The Original Manual for Men's Support Groups © 1992 Bill Kauth

THE FOURTH MEETING

Listening

A joke: Guy is walking down the street with bananas in his ears. Another guy walks up and says: "Hey man, you got bananas in your ears. How come?" The first guy, of course, pulls one of the bananas out and says: "I'm sorry, I couldn't hear you. As you can see, I've got bananas in my ears." End joke.

Most of us walk around at some time with bananas in our ears. Too often we tend not to listen. This problem comes from a variety of reasons, mostly having to do with our own need to feel important. Someone once wisely said, "In relationships, it is better to be interested than interesting." So let's raise our awareness about how we listen.

GROUP STEP 1

Rounds is, as always, the first activity of the meeting. This time the original leader invites the volunteer from last week to lead Rounds and do the summary. This spreads out the leader role, teaches the skills, and begins making the group more "leaderful."

Leader Action 1

Please say: *"As usual, let's start with Rounds. However, as we move toward a leaderful group it is important to continue making the group more democratic. So, I gratefully turn the group over to ___ [his name] ___ ."*

He says: *"Let's do Rounds. What are you feeling now, how has your week been, and my wild card suggestion is ___ [his pick] ___ . Who would like to start?"* After the round he does a summary of the group energy and any agenda that may have emerged.

GROUP STEP 2

Listening: After Rounds has been completed and summarized, the group can move on to this meeting's training activity. Our focus for this meeting is on listening, and we have already emphasized how important it is as a personal communication skill.

Leader Action 2

Introduce your group to Listening Experience #1, which is a five-part process. Say: *"I'm going to take you through a five-part listening activity. Pick a partner, preferably a man with whom you have not yet shared an activity. Sit facing each other. Decide who is going to be A and B."*

Part #1. Say:

"A to B (use his name): Jim, tell me something you are interested in.
B (Jim) does so, tells of something.
A makes no contact, totally ignores and avoids B."

Time of one or two minutes, call stop, and reverse the process, B to A this time. Again time one to two minutes, call stop, and ask for feedback. Say: *"How did it feel to be ignored if you were the speaker, or to do the ignoring?"* (Two or three minutes)

Part #2. Say:

"A to B: Jim, tell me something you are interested in.
B does so.
A listens just long enough to pick up on some key word, then butts in, totally interrupts and takes over the conversation, telling his own thing. B does not have to let himself be taken over."

Time one or two minutes, call stop, and reverse the process, B to A. Same timing, call stop, and ask for feedback. Say: *"How did that one feel to you either way, frustrating, awfully familiar, what?"* (Three or four minutes)

Part #3. Say:

"A: look into the eyes of your partner—don't think, just be there. Experience how it feels just to be with another man with no words getting in the way. Keep breathing.
"B, do the same." (Repeat sentence above)
Time three to five minutes. Call stop. No discussion this time.

Part #4. Say:

"A to B: Jim, tell me something you are interested in.
B does so.
A listens attentively and responds appropriately."
Time two to three minutes, call stop, and reverse B to A.
Same time, call stop.

Part #5. Group discussion:

Ask for feedback. *"What was that like? How did it feel to be together without words? What did you discover it means to 'listen attentively and respond appropriately'?"* (Five to ten minutes)

Take a ten-minute break. Juice and nuts. Talk and listen.

GROUP STEP 3 ▬▬▬▬▬▬▬▬▬▬▬▬▬▬▬▬▬▬▬▬▬▬▬▬▬▬▬

Accurate listening: There are two parties to any communication. Usually the receiver does not get the message in precisely the way the sender meant it. The change of a message during the communication process can be large or small depending on the differences in emotional status, life experiences, needs, and perceptions between receiver and sender. This change is called **distortion** and can lead to misunderstandings. Therefore our goal, as both sender and receiver, is to attempt to make the possibility of distortion as small as possible. An excellent tool for this is called active or "accurate" listening. A visual representation and an accurate listening activity are found on the handout entitled Accurate Listening for the Message. It's at the end of this chapter.

Leader Action 3

Form into small groups of three and review the handout before we start. Whoever did Rounds this meeting might give the following directions to the group. It is an invitation to practice the sequence on the handout.

Say: *"We are going to do this next activity in groups of three. We will take turns in the roles of Sender, Receiver, and Observer. The sender will begin by saying a sentence to the listener that describes an event during the last week and about which he felt something. This is Step 1 on the handout. The other steps follow from there according to the directions. After each exchange is completed, rotate roles so that all three men of your group have an opportunity to practice sending, receiving, and observing in this communication process. Let's begin."*

When all groups have finished rotating, regroup and discuss men's feelings and experiences. Possible topics of discussion could include:

1. How new was this style?
2. Did you improve with practice?
3. What's the value of this style?

GROUP STEP 4

Discussion with listening: Time permitting, the next step for the group is an open discussion on any topic or personal work it chooses. In keeping with integrating the lesson with the discussion, I suggest that this time you combine the listening skill with the discussion in the following way.

Leader Action 4

To begin this activity, say:

"The next activity for the group is our usual discussion process. Maybe we can start with some of the concerns we brought up during Rounds. As an additional way of practicing listening, let's try to reflect back accurately what the man who just spoke said. Then we can add our own comments. This is using 'accurate listening,' but is more spontaneous. It may take a while to get really good at these skills, so now is a good time to make our mistakes in the safety of our group. Who wants to start?"

Pay attention to whether or not the first man to speak reflects back what you have just said. If he does it, acknowledge his quick learning. If he forgets to reflect back, gently correct through an invitation. (Example: *"I heard you saying . . . [whatever he said] . . . and I'd like you first to reflect back what I just said, thanks."*) This activity may seem stilted and unnatural at first. But, with practice, reflective listening behavior will become a very natural skill in your group. It will serve you well as your group matures and conflicts emerge.

Time: Ten or twenty minutes.

GROUP STEP 5

Stretches: You may want to introduce stretches into your group at this point. This tool of stretches really begins to make things happen, as men using the support of the group identify and take action on stuck places in their lives. They are fun, useful, and help bond the group.

Leader Action 5

See Chapter 15 for information on how to make stretches work. Take the time to educate your group about them. Make several photocopies of the **Official Stretch Record** and keep them in a folder or three-ring binder to be held by the new leader for the following week, since it will be his responsibility as part of the group closing to review the stretches.

GROUP STEP 6

Closing the group: After discussion is complete, the new leader closes with The Whip. Anyone can begin, moving around to the right. He says: *"Okay, let's do our closing whip round. How are you feeling now, and is there any unfinished business?"*

Ask for a volunteer leader for the next meeting. Make sure he has the materials he may need.

GROUP STEP 7

Do whatever closing ritual you now use and again say good-bye in a physical way.

Accurate listening for the message

1. Sender

I send the message, then ask receiver to reflect my message.
". . . (message) . . . What do you hear me saying?"

2. Receiver

I listen attentively, acknowledge sender's message.
"I hear you saying . . . (and send it back as I heard it) . . . Is that accurate?"

3. Sender

I listen and acknowledge the accuracy of my message sent back to me.

1) *"That's it."* or 2) *"There's more . . ."*

If there is more, I resend the message with clarification, starting with number 1 until it comes back accurately. Only I, as the sender, know exactly what message I am sending!

4. Observer

I listen, observe, and give feedback to others about their style and behavior.

A newly formed men's group that hasn't quite got the hang of it yet.

THE FIFTH MEETING

Feedback and "work"

At the last meeting we explored the listening process. The other side of the coin is feedback. Together, listening and feedback form communication. Feedback can be defined as accurately letting someone else know our reaction to his actions and the reason for that reaction. It can also include a request for a different action on his part.

Giving others feedback is important for a variety of reasons. Feedback promotes trust by telling others how we feel and letting them know what we are asking of them. Feedback lets others know that we trust them enough to tell them what we think and how we feel.

It is important that a high level of trust be developed within your group. This trust will act to equalize members and bring everyone closer together. That's why I have focused your attention on feedback during this fifth meeting. It's a powerful, supportive way of providing insight and promoting trust.

GROUP STEP 1

I'm going to be a little less directive now about the specifics of activities that take place at every meeting. You probably have developed a number of leadership and communication skills by now and don't need as much direction. As always, begin with Rounds. New leader begins and summarizes.

Leader Action 1

New Rounds volunteer takes over and opens the group meeting.

GROUP STEP 2

How did Rounds go? Probably pretty well. After this meeting, it might be useful for the group to use its feedback skills to tell the various new leaders how they did. This will help a great deal to develop everyone's skills quickly.

At this point, formally introduce a new kind of activity into the group. It is called **"work"** and is simply the opportunity for any man in your group to do his own work. This means many things. Sometimes there is a current conflict a man is dealing with or thinking about. Maybe it is a relationship issue with his children, wife, or parents. Perhaps his business or health is a problem. Something personal is bothering him, and he wants to work on it.

"Work" is essentially what you have already been doing as Rounds issues. Any man may ask for time during Rounds, and his opportunity is added to the agenda for the meeting. It is important to set the time aside for later, or the issue/work may get started during Rounds and take up the whole meeting.

Another way of doing this, if everyone understands the idea of "work" as we are using it, is to have your group do a second round called, "If I was going to 'work,' it would be on _____ ."

Some will want to work, others won't, but everyone will know where the energy is and who is ready. If several men are ready to work at a given meeting, it may be useful to prioritize in some way the level of need: who is really ready now and who can wait. I learned a creative priority method from Eric's group in Chicago. They close their eyes and hold up zero to ten fingers showing their intensity of desire to work. Open eyes and the man with the highest number works first.

Caution: My observation is that as men discover the good feelings of a safe group of other men, they have a tremendous desire to help each other. Unfortunately this "help" too often means giving unwanted advice or confrontation. Because these might actually be counterproductive, so giving a man feedback or challenge without his permission is **not** to be permitted.

The man who wants to work sets the rules! He asks for what he wants. Examples:

> "I just want to tell my story."
> "I want the group to listen without offering solutions."
> "I want feedback."
> "I want advice or suggestions."
> "I want to be challenged or confronted in some way."

He asks for what he wants. The man who wants to work sets the rules!

Leader Action 2

Present the above idea of "work," then perhaps read the Group Step 2 section and discuss it until every man understands the what, why, and how of doing personal "work" in this group. Then, if your group agrees that this is what they want, do the round of "If I was going to work, it would be on _____ ." Do more discussion until all understand and appreciate the possibilities of having this as part of their group. Let them know there may be an opportunity to do some "work" at the end of this meeting.

If your group has definitely decided to do "work" as a part of your meetings, it is imperative that you read the previously stated caution aloud and that it be clearly understood.

GROUP STEP 3

Feedback exercise: Because men may now begin doing "work" in your group, it is especially important that they know how to give **safe and useful feedback.** Mostly we men have been taught how to defend ourselves from each other, often through offensive techniques such as sarcasm and clever put-downs. So we truly need new skills, like accurate feedback—something that will be useful in business as well as in personal relationships. After a review of the materials, let's experiment by using the feedback activity.

Arbitrarily pick a leader for this activity by inviting the man directly to the right of whoever began Rounds to facilitate it. Have feedback handout from end of chapter ready.

Leader Action 3

This is an exercise in learning to give and receive permission for feedback. Say: *"Let's read and discuss the* **Guidelines for giving and receiving effective feedback***."* Take ten minutes or so. *"In this next activity we will be combining listening skills from the last meeting with a new skill—feedback. I want us to do this activity A plus B in groups of three. Let's form combinations that we haven't been in before.*

"Now A says to B, 'You have my permission to tell me something you think I should know. Give me feedback about me.' B does so, and gives A some feedback. Then A says back to B what he heard him saying, to be sure he accurately heard the feedback that was given. Then the third man gives feedback on the skill of giving feedback. When that is complete, change roles and go through it again. When complete, change roles again until each man has played each role.

"Before we start, are there any questions or points about feedback that are unclear? If there are, now would be a good time to bring them up. Okay, let's begin." Five to ten minutes, until each group is complete.

After the activity is finished, get the entire group back together to discuss it. To help discussion along, and because I believe that this is such an important skill, I suggest that everyone make a comment. Please say:

"I want all of us to get back into the circle to discuss this activity. While it's not important for us to go around the circle in order, I want everyone to make a comment about this last activity."

When everyone has commented, open discussion for a while and then move on to the next step.

GROUP STEP 4

Give him the "I" sign: Before going on to your discussion, I want to give you a valuable mini-skill, a silent **feedback tool** for giving each other guidance in using "I" statements and feelings ownership. It is borrowed from sign language. The hand-sign for "I" used by hearing-impaired people is the closed fist against the chest with the little finger up and farthest from the body. Try it out right now. Practice this sign.

In the future, when a group member is making personal statements without owning them, if he is calling himself "you," make this sign to him. It is a quick, useful way of giving **feedback** about "I" statements without interrupting what the man is saying. Give him that instant feedback he needs to correct this long-standing verbal communication error. Give it as a loving gift.

For the next five meetings, I want each of you to be aware of how many times other men noticed you not making "I" statements.

Leader Action 4 _____

Present the above mini-skill so group members have it in their bag of skills. Note to your group that this is a refinement of an "I" statement skill from **our** first meeting.

GROUP STEP 5 ═══════

Awareness, feeling, and interpretation: This exercise is an extension of giving useful feedback and a combination of several skills from the past meetings. It integrates the skills of awareness, feelings, feedback, and self-responsibility.

Leader Action 5 _____

Say: *"Form into pairs and take turns as A and B. Share this three-step process back and forth with your partner. Begin with:*
  1. an **awareness** *observation of your partner, then share*
  2. the **feeling** *brought up by that awareness, and finally*
  3. the **belief** *that (how you have) created the feeling."* (Read the examples.)

Example A
  1. *"When I see you smiling and looking directly at me,*
  2. *I feel glad and warm,*
  3. *because I believe you care about me."*

Example B
  1. *"When I hear you talk on for ten minutes,*
  2. *I sometimes feel annoyed and angry,*
  3. *because I believe that I can't stop you and I want to tell you about me, too."*

Example C
  1. *"When I see your face get red and hear your voice get loud,*
  2. *I feel scared and defensive,*
  3. *because I believe you might hit me like my father did when he looked and sounded like that."*

"Note that the beliefs are your creations, the feelings based on those beliefs are your creations, and you are responsible for those beliefs and feelings. This idea is the key to the exercise. Please begin."

Three to five minutes will be enough time for each man to share one or two observations, feelings, and how he got himself there. After the first partners have done it back and forth a couple of times, stop and have the group discuss the process to clarify how it is being done and guide those who are struggling somewhat in learning it. (Review examples, if necessary.)

Now, change partners and practice again. When each has had an opportunity, change partners one more time, and repeat the process. End and discuss.

GROUP STEP 6

This is the first time your group will be doing "work" as a formal part of the meeting.

Leader Action 6

Open discussion or "work" with men who said during the "If I was going to work" round that they wanted time at this meeting to talk about a personal issue. If a man wants to work on something, set up the time and invite him to let the group know what he wants from them before he begins.

GROUP STEP 7

Closing the group: Review the stretches from last week. Each man checks in on how he did and develops a new stretch to be completed before next meeting. Write them down.

Close the meeting, quick round, perhaps with an appreciation for the man to your right. New leader again closes with The Whip. Anyone can begin, moving around to the right. He says: *"Okay, let's do our closing Whip Round. How are you feeling now, and is there any unfinished business? And give an appreciation to the man on your right. Who wants to begin?"*

Ask for a volunteer leader for next meeting.

GROUP STEP 8

Do whatever closing ritual you now use and again say good-bye in a physical way.

Feedback Credo:
I, and only I, am the sole source of information about how I am reacting to you. Conversely, you, and **only** you, are the sole source of information about how you are reacting to me.
When I speak, I speak only about me, my values, about what I believe works or doesn't work in my life.
My feedback to you is a statement about me.

Guidelines for giving and receiving effective feedback

The following guidelines make the process simple:

1. **Caring and respect:** The most important consideration in the feedback process is that it be done with caring and respect. All feedback is "positive feedback" if it is given with caring.

2. **Ask permission:** Before giving feedback ask for permission. (Example: "May I give you some feedback?" or "I want to tell you something about how I see you, is that okay?") Wait for receptiveness to your feedback, then proceed.

3. **Giving feedback:** Giving feedback is like a fun-house mirror. I can reflect back my observations and feelings about another's behavior. All of these reflections will be on the wavy mirror that I am. The question is how to be truly useful to others.

   The following may help us give feedback more effectively to others:

   1. **Speak to behavior:** Effective feedback is the reporting of observable behavior. It is not interpretations, judgments, hunches, solutions, or analysis.
   2. **Be specific and direct:** It is more effective to report exact behavior than general impressions. (Example: "I've noticed that you have been quiet all evening," rather than "You seem moody tonight.")
   3. **Share the effect:** It is helpful to let men know what followed the behavior. (Example: "When I saw your face get red and heard your voice rise, I felt scared.")
   4. **Be immediate:** Give feedback as soon after something happens as possible. Later it is hard to recall and it loses impact.
   5. **Be brief:** Effective feedback is generally short, simple, and to the point.

4. **Receiving feedback:** If you want to know what people think or feel about you or your behavior, ask them. This is a risky step for most people. In truth it is usually less scary to ask than to continue wondering and worrying. So when you feel ready, take the risk and ask for feedback.

   Whether or not you "hear" the feedback you receive is affected by many things: your general openness, the day, the language used, the effectiveness of the feedback giver, feeling of security, trust of the giver, readiness, etc.

   An important thing to know about receiving feedback is that **you don't have to do anything with it**. You do not have to change if you hear it. So, trust that the feedback is given with caring and decide if it is useful or not. Keep what is useful to know about yourself and discard or store the rest.

   The following may help you hear more and use the feedback you get:

   1. **Concentrate on listening:** You do not need to respond. Often it is better not to respond immediately. Let it wash over you and take what you can use.
   2. **Wait:** Hold off a bit and let what was said to you really sink in. Give it time.
   3. **Sum up:** Repeat the gist of what was said to you out loud. (Example: "Sounds like you think that sometimes when I smile, I'm feeling afraid and it confuses you.")
   4. **Get clear:** Ask for clarification if you need it.
   5. **Don't swallow it:** It may have little or nothing to do with you.
   6. **Don't let yourself get overloaded:** If you're feeling overwhelmed, say "stop."

THE SIXTH MEETING

Hassles and conflict

You may have noticed some interesting things going on in your group during the past few weeks, things like hassles and conflict. Perhaps you have even felt uncomfortable sometimes about a certain man or the group in general. Chances are, if you read the previous couple of sentences and felt a reaction like "Yeah!" you are experiencing some conflicts. GREAT!

Conflict in the various stages of a group is to be expected and welcomed. **Expected**, because it is natural for men who are together to have some creative differences. In fact these differences are what will keep your group alive and growing. **Welcomed**, because it can help the men of your group to develop trust for each other and to experience the successful resolution of these differences. It is a demonstration that we can have conflict and still remain in the company of men.

Too often, we men were raised by women. Dad was not there for us, and we grew up not really knowing ourselves or other men. This has taken the form of fearing and distrusting other men. Sometimes we get close enough to somebody to have a "fight," a conflict, and if it doesn't work out quickly, we give up that friend. Too bad, because the possibility for deep friendship was just starting. It seems that sometimes men have to "fight" with each other to get close.

The creative resolution of conflict can open the door to intimacy. The activities in this session are designed to bring to the surface some of these hassles and conflicts, show you ways to resolve them, and give you opportunities to practice the communication skills you have learned.

GROUP STEP 1

You don't need my guidance anymore to do Rounds, so do it.

Leader Action 1

New leader opens group. Then move to the next activity.

GROUP STEP 2

This is the highest risk activity you will have done and is designed to demonstrate dramatically the value of taking the risk to give honest feedback. This activity is likely to bring conflicts to the surface and is focused on personal trust levels within your group. It uses all of the communication skills you have been practicing. The ultimate goal is to build some bridges and tear down some walls between men. Whoever is the leader for this activity, it is best to **be well prepared ahead of time.**

Leader Action 2

After Rounds is complete, say:

"This activity will be more risky than the others and is deliberately designed to be so. Take the risk and reap the reward. Take a look around your group; be aware of each man here, including me. You have spent the last five meetings getting to know these men and you have formed impressions. Now in your own mind, silently choose the man you trust the most (pause one minute). Now choose the man you trust the least or are least comfortable with (pause one minute). This is intended as a forced choice, so it is a given that you may trust these men more than most men outside of this group. Pick two!

"Now that you have chosen both men, the next step will be to share with both men—the man you trust the most and the man you trust the least—that you have chosen them.

"If you are chosen by another man to receive the feedback that you are either most or least trusted, the appropriate response is 'thank you' and nothing more. There will be an opportunity later. So for now simply respond with 'thank you,' meaning 'I acknowledge your courage in taking this risk.'

"Now speak directly to both men; tell each that you either trust him the most or the least. You may say why if you want to, or you may choose to hold that information. This will be done in random order. Who wants to begin?"

After all the men have shared both their most and least trust, discuss it for **as long as the group needs**. Say:

"Okay, it sounds like everyone has shared. Good work! Everyone take a deep breath. Now let's discuss what you felt. Stay with feelings. How was it for you to share that information? If you were chosen most or least, how did it feel to be chosen? How did it feel not to be chosen? Are there any clarifying questions you need to ask any other man? Now is the time, the floor is open."

During the discussion make sure these three points are made

1. Let the discussion process go on for fifteen minutes or even a half hour before pointing out that the value of high-risk feedback when done in a caring and positive way can **build bridges and take down walls**! By then it will be obvious to all that this is what has just happened and the group is actually bonded more closely for having taken the risks. If any man seems particularly scared or stunned by the process, invite him to share his feelings until he is clear of confusion and knows he is a valued part of the group.

2. Point out the concept of projection, that we see in others what lives in us. Often our distrust/discomfort with a certain man indicates that there is something about him that is part of us we may not yet know much about. So this man is a special gift to us in terms of learning more about ourselves. Look closely at that man you chose as "least," get to know him well.

3. Definition of conflict: "I want one thing and you want another." I want

to go camping and you want to go surfing. I want vanilla and you want chocolate. I want to save and you want to spend. Life is filled with conflict every day. The successful resolution of conflict usually involves some level of self-revealing. This creates intimacy. Which is why often just being with someone for a number of months or years will lead to some intimacy. What we are doing in our group is deliberately accelerating the process. If we can do it successfully here, we can do it better in our world at large.

4. Discussion lasts as long as the group needs.

Author comment

I consider this trust process to be the turning point in a men's group. It is my experience that men often have to fight, to engage in conflict, to bond as friends. There is something about seeing the other man operating under fire, in the heat of battle, that creates a trust bond for men. Perhaps it is one of those moments when we get to see each other in a pure emotional presence, telling the bare truth. It is also a demonstration of courage, in that I want as my friend a man who can face off with me, who is equal to me in personal power. If he is too scared to stand with me toe to toe, he probably won't be able to stand firmly at my side, either. This courage and personal power can be learned, which is one of the great opportunities your men's group gives you. It is a part of manhood that can be learned only with other men, and working together with trust and mutual support is a lot easier than doing it on you own out in the world. So I want this high-risk, trust-identification activity to be for you a precedent for future opportunities to risk with other men.

"Hey! You guys! Let's build some bridges!"

Break. Take some time to relax.

GROUP STEP 3

Work or discussion: Your group may be ready to go on to "work" from opening rounds, or they may want a lighter discussion. Find out what the group wants.

The purpose of conflict is to reveal the mystery.

GROUP STEP 4

Stretches: If your group is doing stretches, I strongly suggest that this week's stretches include making contact (example: getting together for lunch) with the man you chose as "least." Some amazing gifts and group cohesion can result from these personal contacts.

GROUP STEP 5

Closing rounds. Any unfinished business and how do you feel now? Pick a new leader for next meeting.

The Courage in Conflict
Without honest conflict, a group dies of a disease
we call confluence,
which is everybody making "nice-nice."

THE SEVENTH MEETING

The power and pleasure of play

Men play? Pretty outrageous concept, isn't it?

Not at all. It has even been suggested that our playfulness is the reason women keep us around. Lots of us were taught to keep our noses to the grindstone and shoulders to the wheel, etc. Which of course makes it tough to stand up straight, much less have any fun. However, that playful boy lives in all of us, waiting for an opportunity to leap out.

So as a delightful change of pace and relief from some of the tension of the last few meetings, let's focus this meeting on playing together. I want you to know there are some very different activities that are fun for any group of men of any age. So think of this as an invitation to play.

You can make up your own games or go to the books. There are books available that include hundreds of playful noncompetitive games with great names: Blob Tag, Vampire, and Group Safari. **_New Games_**, by the New Games Foundation, is one source. Another is **_Playfair_**, by Matt Weinstein and Joel Goodman, which includes playful activities for men of any age to enjoy so we can become the spontaneous beings we all have as part of ourselves. Playing together might also mean any of the activities in Chapter 19.

Playing together will help you discover things about each other and yourselves you may not have seen before. You will know that they (and you) are successful when smiles and giggles abound.

The directions for this group meeting are very simple.

GROUP STEP 1

A variation of Rounds.

Leader Action 1

New leader begins with Rounds, as usual. The wild-card topic might be: "My favorite game."`

GROUP STEP 2

Get serious about this play stuff: The creative use of play can be a powerful way to work with your men's group. All of us have probably formed a large part of our self-concept through our play-related activities. Play is powerful because it teaches us that we are powerful. Play is pleasurable because it directly stimulates our pleasure centers by lowering our stress, enhancing our creativity, increasing our sensitivity, and reinforcing our sense of group membership.

However, games and play that require competition, winning, and "one-upmanship" benefit only those who are stronger, smarter, or more talented than the rest of us.

While it is clear that there is a demand and value for competitive activities—for example, as an alternative to war—it is also clear that in terms of growthful participation they benefit a minority and force many of us to become spectators. New games (as I broadly define them) are playful activities that allow everyone to participate and be a winner—games that allow success, maximize direct participation, positive cooperation, and trust, and build self-esteem, confidence, and mutual respect.

Some groups designate every fourth or so meeting as a play meeting, by design. All members agree and know that once each month (or whenever) the group decides it is playtime. One member will volunteer ahead of time to arrange the following month's playtime.

So, before you go on to other "important, serious stuff," ask one member to volunteer or be chosen to direct a future play activity. Do it now, so it is not forgotten.

Leader Action 2

As a group, choose one or two games you brought up in Rounds or took from the books I mentioned. You might begin with the games for individuals and work your way up to full-group games. Each member might direct at least one game. (There are enough in the books for everyone.)

GROUP STEP 3

Work, discuss, or play some more.

GROUP STEP 4

Finish with closing rounds, as usual.

"There's a Mr. Iron John on the line, sir . . . he wants to know if you can come out and play."

THE EIGHTH MEETING

Who are we now and where are we going?

At this point it is useful for your group to evaluate its progress and process so far. The group will then need to make a decision—either to continue with more training, using some of the structured exercises or topics in Chapters 16 and 17, or go with the flow. There is a tendency for groups to get stuck at this point in a familiar pattern of structured learning experiences and be afraid to "trust the process" of going with whatever comes up for men in the group. So the question is: "Do we need more training or are we ready to go for a few meetings without a formal agenda?"

I suggest that your group make the decision by consensus. Consensus is reached when every man agrees to support the group decision. It may not have been what a man originally wanted, but as the discussion went on he got a feeling for what the group wanted and simply decided he would also support it. When a man feels strongly, for whatever reason, that the direction he wants is important, he fights for it. Sometimes the group may go his way and sometimes not. This decision-making process may be more time consuming, but I believe it is important. Consensus ensures every man's full input until the decision is made by the full group.

Consensus statement: We as a group will engage in a discussion and/or conflict in which every man has had an opportunity to be heard in order to reach an agreement supported by every man here.

One of the reasons this works is because often the passion of a man pushing for his direction will convince the rest of the group. There is a tendency to trust a man's passion because we know that his idea will either work or it won't, and that he is responsible for it either way. So if he is that willing to put his "buns on the line," we are likely to be willing to support his idea.

The gathering of information will likely be useful in deciding how to proceed with your group. Honestly evaluating the group together will make it easier to decide on the next step.

GROUP STEP 1
Opening Rounds.

Leader Action 1
New leader opens with Rounds.

GROUP STEP 2

The group evaluation process: Evaluating your group is an ongoing process that you will do consciously and unconsciously many times. This process can take many forms, depending on your needs and the reasons for evaluation. I believe that the single most important reason for you, as an individual, to evaluate your group is so that you know when the group **is** and **is not** meeting your needs. I also believe it is important to make this evaluation process as conscious an act as possible so that you can make decisions about your behavior in the group and share the information with this group of warm, supportive men. Chapters 27 and 28 may be useful for your group in this process.

On the next page is a form that can help you in assessing your group. I suggest that you duplicate this form and use it at regular intervals throughout the life of your group.

Leader Action 2

Share the above information with your group, fill out the evaluation forms, and discuss with feelings. Make a decision by consensus.

GROUP STEP 3

Work, discuss, or play.

GROUP STEP 4

Close the group. Stretches, whip, and closing.

*"All right Ted, I **will** be honest with you. I really **do** love this car more than my wife!"*

Men's support group assessment form

Content

1. Do you think that you knew what your goals were when we began?

2. Were these goals reached?

3. Do you believe you were aware of the goals that other members brought to the group?

4. Were these goals reached?

5. Were any discussion topics or activities particularly difficult or troublesome for you?

6. What changes or additions in **Content** would you suggest for future group meetings?

Process

1. Did all group members willingly participate in all group topics/activities?

2. If not, check the most probable causes, in your opinion.
   a. A majority of group members chose to discuss other matters.
   b. Too much time was spent on one activity.
   c. Group members brought up personal concerns.

3. Do you feel good about how the group is presently functioning?

4. If not, how would you change the group process?

5. Do you feel comfortable with how we men are relating to each other?

6. If not, what would you change about yourself or the other men?

7. Do you feel satisfied with the way you are helping guide the group?

8. If not, what would you like to change about the way you are helping?

A Circle of Men: The Original Manual for Men's Support Groups © 1992 Bill Kauth

PART THREE
ACTIVITIES AND CHALLENGES FOR YOUR GROUP

"By all means let us cherish the traditional sports for their many beauties, their unplumbed potential, and for the certainty they afford. But we have signed no long-term contract to suffer their extremes. The time has come to move on, to create new games with new rules more in tune with the times, games in which there are no spectators and no second-string players, games for a whole family and a whole day, games in which aggression fades into laughter—new games."
—George Leonard, *The Ultimate Athlete*

STRETCHES AND GOALS

One of the single most powerful ways you can serve each other in your group is through what I have been calling "stretches." These are short-term, weekly (or as often as your group meets) goals—set by each member of your group with the full support of everyone else.

I call them stretches because they are intended to go beyond your reach—into areas that involve some fear or anxiety. They could involve making a phone call to someone you are afraid to call, completion/cleaning up a relationship, exercising a couple times a week, cleaning the basement (which has been put off for two years), confronting someone you care about, etc. They are **very** personal.

Some rules and guidelines

Logistics: The stretches need to be recorded in writing. So an ongoing volunteer who is willing to take the notes and bring them to the next meeting is needed. (See "Official Stretch Record.") Make plenty of photocopies and keep them in a three-ring binder or pocket folder.

Process: Each man in turn presents the stretch he thinks will be a challenge during the time until the next meeting. The group listens, and if anyone thinks it is not an adequate stretch, the man is invited to go further and refine it in some way—or choose a different stretch with more challenge. This is akin to "tough love," not letting your friend "wimp out" or sell himself short.

Qualities of appropriate stretches
1. Personally important, significant in your life.
2. Emotionally loaded, some feeling connected with this activity.
3. Behaviorally specific, measurable. (Not "I'm gonna exercise this week," rather, "I'm gonna run or ride my bike fifteen minutes each day.")

Near the end of the meeting (leave fifteen to twenty minutes) the recorder reads, in turn, each member's stretch from the last meeting and asks if he made it. He shares whether he made it and whatever else he wants to share about what he learned from the experience. The group can have some say as to whether it was done in full or not.

Possible responses to making or not making the stretch
If the stretch was made, other members can make some acknowledgment. If the stretch was not made, the response is not to be chastising or punishing in any way. This is, after all, a "support" group!

My own men's group found that if a stretch was not made, a token "donation" to a "group kitty" stimulated a lot more fun and intention. There is something about money that seems to help a man hold his stretch more clearly in mind until he gets it handled. If your group chooses this reminder system, the amount is yours to decide, perhaps a dollar or two. However, we've found that five dollars cranks up the ante. A recorder holds the money until it reaches a set amount, then it is given philanthropically or used for a party or whatever **your** group decides. Caution: We also found our group unconsciously slipping into some old punitive shaming patterns with this model. In their grossest form they sounded like "You didn't make it, pay, sucker!"

Fortunately, unconditional support is possible. After considerable pondering and wanting their stretch reminder to be totally positive, Bob Walter's men's group created the "Joy Drum." Many of our local groups drum before their meetings (see Chapter 26 on rituals). His group has a member, a drum maker, who made a group drum, which is at every meeting. Now, when a man makes his stretch, he gets to beat the group drum to the cheers of the rest of his group.

*"Oh yeah? Well, my dad's more **spiritual** than your dad!"*

Official stretch record

Date today: _____   Next meeting date: _____

	Name	Stretch	Made It?
1.			
2.			
3.			
4.			
5.			
6.			
7.			
8.			
9.			
10.			
11.			

16

STRUCTURED LEARNING ACTIVITIES

On the next few pages are several proven learning activities that you may want to use in your men's group. These activities can give a sense of security to a new group by providing some "recipes" to be used when needed. The best activities, of course, are the ones that you will invent, because they serve your group's individual needs. So, until you are able to invent your own, I invite you to try out some of these creative experiences. Have fun!

BRIEF ACTIVITIES TO RAISE THE SELF-ESTEEM OF THE MEN IN YOUR GROUP

1. *The Nourishing Game*—Every man in the group takes a turn telling the others something that he has done to make himself feel happy or good about himself.
2. *Strength Bombardment*—One man is chosen (with his permission) or volunteers to hear, for one minute, wonderful, excellent, positive qualities about himself described by the rest of the group.
3. *The Bragging Game*—A man (or every man) has to tell some of his virtues and/or accomplishments for thirty to forty-five seconds. At the end of that time, everyone applauds the speaker.
4. *Make up your own!*

INTRODUCE YOUR DAD

Purpose: To explore who we imagine our fathers to be, our feelings about them, any unfinished business, and how we may be like them.

Process: Each man takes a turn introducing his father to the group, as if Dad were actually there. He can give facts and details and/or his feelings about Dad. Because this is a highly charged area for all of us, this process could take several weeks. Make this known at the beginning so men can plan to take all the time they may need.

If in the course of the introduction a man feels a need to work with something that has come up, he asks for what he needs, just like "work" in group meetings.

Be your father: A playful variation to be used before, during, or after the introductions. Set up a cocktail party, a board meeting, or maybe a Sunday dinner scenario in which every man plays his father. Get agreement to do it, set the scene, and go at it for ten or fifteen minutes. When you are finished, be aware of any feelings and similarities between you and your father. Discuss.

Note: How men relate to their fathers is likely the same way they relate to men in the group—another fertile topic for discussing and sharing feelings.

SONGS OF AFFIRMATION

Purpose: To share part of who I am and how I got to be me through the medium of music.

Process: Everyone brings to the group, as requested the previous week, a song, either written out or in the form of a recording. The song or piece of music is to be one that is affirming, liberating, or special in some way. Each man has an opportunity to share his music by either playing it or reading the words aloud, then talking about what significance it has had on his life. Note: This will also work splendidly with poems.

MY DICK SPEAKS

Purpose: To open up playfully the area of sexuality, get rid of shame, and learn to accept more lovingly an often maligned part of us.

Process: If men have pet names for their penises, use those names (I have a friend who speaks fondly about Big Wally, and what we know from Big Wally is that Doug calls him that to make Big Wally feel better). If they don't already have names, give them names now. Then have each man tell a tale from his dick's point of view.

"Hi, I'm _____ , I belong to _____ , and let me tell you . . ."

What it feels like to be _____'s dick.

What _____ has done with me.

How _____ has treated me.

About embarrassing moments I've had with _____ .

What _____ has done to me over the years.

About some conflicts I've had with _____ .

Read the list and invite each man to tell a tale from his dick's point of view. Do not refer back to the list.

CIRCLE-RIGHT AND CIRCLE-LEFT

Purpose: Provides an opportunity to receive some positive and nurturing feedback. Then a chance to experience owning the positives. Also an opportunity to learn what curiosity other men have about us.

Process: Each man in the group has a blank piece of paper and writes his name at the top. Papers are then passed to the left and everyone has thirty seconds to write something positive about the man whose name is on the paper. Describe a quality, attribute, or feeling you have about that man. Continue passing the paper to the left until it returns to its owner.

Now turn it over and pass it to the right. Each man has thirty seconds to write one thing that he is curious about regarding the owner of the paper. Continue passing the papers to the right until they return home.

At this point any man who wishes to share may read all the positives, translating them into the first person. (I have a handsome nose, I'm very witty, I'm real smart.)

Also, any man who wants to may respond to just one of the things someone was curious about.

Caution: Avoid pressuring anyone into sharing the curiosity items. Respect each man's right not to participate; he may have learned plenty from just the question or statement.

Materials: paper and writing implements.

I AM . . .

Purpose: Exploration and acknowledgment of self and others. Gives each man an opportunity to know himself in the rich variety of identities he ascribes to himself, within a safe situation of receiving unconditional acknowledgment.

Process: Best setting is warm, comfortable, and quiet, with dim lighting.

1. Choose partners. Decide who is A and who is B. Sit face to face, maintain eye contact as much as you are comfortable with, and remember to BREATHE.
2. A begins by saying to B: "Tell me who you are." B responds with the statement, "I am _____ ," filling in whatever he believes he is at that moment.
3. A listens attentively with no indication of approval or disapproval and acknowledges by saying, "Thank you." And again saying, "Tell me who you are."
4. The process continues with B again responding, "I am _____ ," and A acknowledging with, "Thank you," for at least three to five minutes.
5. Switch roles: B begins with: "Tell me who you are," A responding with "I am _____ ," B acknowledging with "Thank you," and so on for at least three to five minutes.
6. Thank your partner and change partners. Decide who is A and B and begin.

Note: This experience can continue for as long as you wish. I recommend changing partners three times, about one half hour total time.

Repeat this exercise often, every month or so. You may notice some interesting changes in your definitions of yourself over time. Group feedback on this experience could be useful, but don't "overhash" it. Let silence allow your new self-perceptions to sink in.

1-2-1-4-1 (MAN-TO-MINUTE)

Purpose: To provide every man in the group a brief individual contact with every other man in the group while focused on a high-risk topic. This will increase the level of openness, risk, and sharing in the group.

Process: The leader and/or whole group decides on an opening phrase, such as:

1. My first impression of you was . . .
2. One thing I want to tell you is . . .
3. What I like about you is . . .
4. What I like about me is . . .
5. What I don't want you to know about me is . . .
6. What I could learn from you is . . .
7. My apprehension about you is . . .
8. What I see in you that I see in me is . . .
9. You remind me of . . .
10. (Create your own)

The group pairs up and decides who of each pair will go first. Timekeeper rings bell or "ringer-dinger," and one man in each pair speaks, starting with opening phrase chosen. The other man listens for one minute. Bell rings. Roles reverse, listener speaks, other listens.

When the bell rings again everyone chooses a new partner and repeats above process at one-minute intervals with successive rings of the bell. Repeat until everyone has spoken and listened to everyone else for one minute. (The timekeeper/bell ringer can rotate or be the same man throughout.) Everyone participates.

Caution: Be sure everyone is willing to play and has agreed on the opener.

Materials: If a bell is not available, we have found that a wineglass and spoon work better than an ashtray and ballpoint pen as a substitute ringer-dinger.

MAKING CONTACT

Purpose: To enhance mutual trust. Each of us at some time has probably used a negative method for making contact with other men. It is important to be aware of how we contact others before we can change. There is awareness learning in both giving and receiving the feedback.

Process:

1. Sitting in a circle, each man looks at every other man in the group and

gets a feeling about how he can make contact with that man.

2. One at a time, each man in the group makes a direct verbal statement to each of the other members in the group, beginning each statement with: "I can make contact with you by . . ." (Example: "Bob, I can make contact with you by smiling when you look at me" or "Joe, I can make contact with you by criticizing what you say.") The man receiving the statement responds with "thank you."

3. Continue this process until every man has had a chance to tell everyone else how he can make contact with him.

Note: As best you can, do not place negative judgments on the statements but look at them as valuable pieces of new awareness. It is important to acknowledge the risk that each man takes in his sharing process. The response of "thank you" is short for "thank you for your courage in trusting me enough to share your truth."

Alternatives: Use the same process but substitute the statement, "I can avoid contact with you by. . . ."

I SEEM TO BE . . . BUT . . .

Purpose: To give us an opportunity to explore how we seem to be and how we actually are with other men. We are supported in this process through receiving unconditional acknowledgment for disclosing a "shadow" part of ourselves that is often hidden to others.

Process:

1. Divide into pairs. Sit face-to-face. Maintain eye contact and remember to breathe. Decide who will be A and who will be B.

2. A begins: "I seem to be . . . but I . . ." B listens attentively and acknowledges each statement with "thank you." (Example: "I seem to be a quiet guy but actually I talk a lot." Or "I seem to be bored, but I'm only waiting." Or "I seem to have lots of friends, but I'm really lonely sometimes.")

3. This process continues for two to three minutes.

4. Switch. B now repeats, "I seem to be . . . but . . ." and A acknowledges each disclosure with "thank you."

5. When both men have shared, provide three to four minutes to discuss between them what they learned.

6. Change partners and repeat.

7. Full group discussion and feedback as needed and wanted.

EMOTIONAL SHARING

Purpose: To use the group support and safety to open up emotionally and perhaps get to know some emotionally hidden parts of ourselves.

Process: After you have gotten the group's support in sharing this experience, let them know you will be leading a brief guided journey, followed by time to work with whatever may come up. It is all voluntary. Prepare them to begin.

"Sit quietly with your eyes closed and relax. (Give group time to do so.)

Now let your mind drift to something that you experienced last week, some time when you felt fear, anger, sadness, joy, or shame. Be with that experience. Feel it in your body as you remember the experience. You know in your body if that experience is complete or not. When we express the feeling, it does not linger. When we say what we have to say it does not get stuck in our throat. If you have a sense that the feeling experience is unfinished, you may want to bring it out here in the safety of your group.

"Now as it feels right, you will have an opportunity to share that experience, and if you want to work with it, ask the group to help you complete the emotional experience."

The group listens to what each man wants and helps him complete the feeling experience. This may mean just talking about the experience or it may involve tears or some expression of anger. If grief is emerging, some physical contact and reassurance may be useful. If a man is experiencing anger, perhaps growling, twisting a towel, or pounding a pillow may be a way for him to get his body engaged enough to let the anger emerge, so that he can come to feel safe with that feeling in himself.

PROJECTION FANTASY

Purpose: To understand the dynamic of "projection" in communication and interpersonal relations. What we see in others says a lot about who we are.

Process: This is a silent exercise involving pairs and a leader who is solo. This is an exercise for the imagination. Remember to maintain eye contact with your partner and BREATHE.

1. Decide who will lead the exercise; the rest will divide into pairs. The leader will sit near the group so that he can speak in a steady, comforting voice and be heard by all. The pairs sit comfortably face-to-face.

2. The leader will ask the participants to look at each other in silence and answer these questions in their minds as they picture the man in front of them:

   "Look at your partner and imagine
     What was it like for this man growing up?
     Was this man happy? Sad?
     How many brothers and sisters did this man have?
     Was he an only child, a middle child, the baby?
     How did this man feel about his family position?
     What were his favorite games?
     Was this man athletic? Shy? Silly? Bookish?
     Did this man play a musical instrument? Which one?
     What was he most afraid of as a boy?
     What did he do when afraid?"

   Be creative and expand on this list, adding your own questions.

   Following is a list of additional topics:
     School experiences
     Favorite subjects in school

Favorite toys
Parents and relatives
Friends
Pets
Other life events and your partner's feelings about them

Plan for three to five minutes total time and pause briefly between each question. Using a soothing voice helps men to get good visual images and to stay relaxed.

3. The men in pairs imagine the answers to the leader's questions for the man opposite them. "Picture that man in your mind as you imagine how he was."
4. Discussion: After the exercise, share with your partner what your fantasy of him was and how that image relates to you and your history. Was it similar? Different? Was it a projection of what you wanted and didn't get or have? How did your fantasy of the other man reflect you and what you wanted?
5. Switch partners and change leaders. Repeat two or three times.
6. Full group discussion if it is wanted.

STRENGTH EMPOWERMENT

Purpose: To enhance mutual appreciation and awareness of our own and other men's strengths.

Process:

1. Divide into pairs and decide who will go first.
2. First man takes two minutes to tell what he considers to be his personal strengths, including what he thinks he does well, likes about himself, and what he thinks others like about him.
3. Second man then "bombards" partner with any observations he has about numero uno's strengths and personal assets. (Three to five minutes)
4. As first man receives a piece of feedback he responds by
   a. paraphrasing the feedback, and
   b. stating what he thinks his partner means and clarifying the meaning. In other words, using "active listening" skills.
5. Reverse roles and repeat the process.

Note: Native American people might see this process as learning to "walk the beauty way" in the area of men's personal power. What we can see in another man lives in us.

GOOD BOY–BAD BOY

Purpose: Awareness of early experiences, family roles, and how we may have carried them into adulthood.

Process:

1. Choose a partner you want to know better and decide who is A and who is B. Sit face-to-face. A will be the good boy and B the bad boy. Now tell each other all about yourselves, what you are like, and the specific things you do. For example: "I'm a good boy, I always wipe the dirt off my shoes before I come into the house, and I never get angry. I'd never do the awful things you do." "I'm a bad boy, I like knives, strangling cats, making fires, and fighting. I always leave the toilet seat up. And I hate all stupid rules."

2. As you continue your conversation, be aware of your own hesitations, volume, expressiveness, etc. (Four or five minutes) Switch roles. (Four or five minutes)

3. When you are finished, sit and quietly absorb your experiences. How did you feel in each role? What kinds of things did you say in each role? Which role felt more comfortable? How did you interact with the opposing role played by your partner? Did you discover anything new about yourself in either role? What were you most aware of in your partner's expressions?

4. Now share with each other your feeling about your own experiences and your impressions of each other.

Note: There are other sets of opposites you might want to experiment with: parent-child, teacher-student, black-white, husband-wife, employer-employee, strong-weak, emotional-unemotional, sane-crazy, hawk-dove, honest-dishonest, etc.

You might also want to experiment by doing this process with eyes closed, to focus on voice tone and body awareness.

"Tell the Royal Prince that if he doesn't stop bouncing that golden ball off the throne room wall I'm going to tan his royal butt!"

TOPICS AND ISSUES FOR DISCUSSION

"Men's issues" are whatever men are talking about. The following are some of the topics we seem to focus on in our growth and empowerment process. Some are riskier than others. When you introduce a topic, I suggest starting with a round in which each man states what is at risk for him in exploring this topic. This will get the discussion quickly to a feeling level as fears and secrets are laid out up front.

It will probably work best to block out a specific amount of time (it might be thirty minutes, or two hours) for any specific topic, then negotiate more time if that is what the group wants.

1. **Courage.** How do I know I'm doing my personal best? Story of a time I acted courageously.

2. **Fathers and sons.** We all had one and we all are one. What are our feelings about our dads and ourselves?

3. **Mothers and women.** What are our feelings about them? Are there correlations between Mom and the women we choose to be with?

4. **Integrity and manhood.** How do I know or will I know when I'm a man? How does a man know when he is "in integrity" and has integrated all the parts of himself?

5. **Jokes and humor.** Is there a message here? Do we cover our feelings with humor? Is it a club we use to beat each other? Shame?

6. **Sexuality.** Huge confusion with intimacy. Is it mostly fantasy for us? What truth can we tell that's not covered by bravado?

7. **Spirituality.** Definition? How do we find our connection with spirit/God/universe?

8. **Fathering.** First emotional experience of being a father. What does nurturing mean? Can we distinguish discipline from punishment? Step-parenting.

9. **Violence.** What is the definition? If we were to own our violence, what would it be? Can we learn to live without violence? Is it true that punishment never works?

10. **Money and net worth.** Is money really that important to us as men? How much attention do we give to financial security? Do we measure another man by the bulge of his wallet?

11. **Penises.** Do we measure our self-worth by the imagined lack of bulge in our pants? Penis size is a major identity issue. We joke about it, but can we talk about it?

12. **Power.** Some men would rather talk about sex and money than power. Where does power come from and how do we use it? Is power important, mandatory, corrupting, embarrassing?

13. **Shame.** Most men feel it and never talk about it, because shame is always secret. Maybe your group is the safe place to bring it into the light.

14. **Separation.** Saying good-bye, styles, feelings. Alone versus lonely.

15. **Ancestors.** We need roots. Who were our grandfathers and great-grandfathers and so on back? What were their names? What did they do? Find out and share.

The "Freedom from Shame" final exam, exercise #26, "Mommy Shit."

GETTING UN-STUCK

Creative challenges

The following are some **stuck situations** that may be observed by a man in the group (not you, of course) who becomes aware of himself as doing one of the behaviors in the first column. Or it may be noticed by another man who cares enough to bring it to his attention. This is to be done lovingly, with permission, and as an invitation to take the **challenge assignment** in the second column. These experimental challenges can be great fun when done with the caring support of your group. They are also useful as possible stretches (see Chapter 15).

Stuck situations	Challenge assignments
1. Man is new and does not feel part of group.	1. He becomes the group host.
2. Man feels isolated in group.	2. Big brother provided by member of the group.
3. Man is overt or covert rebel.	3. Becomes group rebel, openly. Exaggerate.
4. Man doesn't know how to be silly or play.	4. Do specific silly things in public suggested by group members.
5. Man does not understand or refuses to take responsibility for feelings, thoughts, etc.	5. Another group member takes responsibility for his feelings and thoughts.
6. Man not in touch with own feelings, too intellectualized.	6. Blindfold and/or ask for one-word feelings.
7. Man unaware of others' feelings, too self-involved.	7. He becomes the feelings observer.
8. Man is pleaser—can never say no to anyone.	8. Be uncooperative and even nasty.
9. Man has many expectations of others.	9. He turns them into demands.
10. Man constantly asking questions.	10. Turn all questions into statements.
11. Man is chronic advice-giver.	11. He gets feedback from group on how they feel about getting the advice.
12. For various reasons, man is unable to express negative feelings.	12. He becomes group critic leading to obnoxious-bastard status.
13. Man doesn't know how to fight verbally with others.	13. Role-play arguments with group members followed by arguments with important people.

14. Man is very private or guarded.
15. Man unable to show warm feelings.

16. Man wants to be perfect or above criticism.
17. Man is needy for emotional support or contact with people, but will not reach out to anyone.
18. Man feels shallow, doubts ability to use brain.
19. Man is self-involved and overly impressed with his own greatness.
20. Man never listens to criticism, but immediately gets defensive or attacking.
21. Man is afraid to show weakness or softness.

22. Man doesn't really understand members of opposite sex.
23. Man has a limited or undefined value system.

24. Man doesn't know what people outside of group think of him.
25. Man doesn't know how to have an equal relationship.

26. Man has limited ways of relating in groups of people.
27. Man has never experienced satisfaction and fulfillment from any work.
28. Man not comfortable talking about sex.
29. Man directly or indirectly controls and dominates others.
30. Man expects special treatment from the world.

14. Share with each group member one secret about himself.
15. Whenever he has warm feelings, actually touch other man in some safe way.

16. Do stupid or clumsy things in the group, later in public.
17. Ask for something of an emotional nature from three men during the week.
18. Present five-minute news editorial in group.
19. Group superstar. Tell group about past and present greatness.
20. Listen to the content of all criticism. Understand the nature of negative feedback.
21. Whenever he is feeling weak or vulnerable, tell other men about those feelings.

22. Interview three to five women and get to know them as people.
23. Make all decisions and choices of behavior on the basis of what he can respect.

24. Ask five people he knows well to tell him honestly what positive and negative qualities he has.
25. Come on with the same attitude as other men present to him—dominant, submissive, or equal.

26. Play roles that man is unfamiliar with in group.
27. Make something original without assistance from anyone.

28. Make up personal sexual fantasies and read them in group.
29. Group dictator. Exaggerate.

30. He becomes the group prince. Exaggerate.

31. Man exploring the kind of man he wants to be.

31. Come to group dressed up and ready to portray different social roles.

32. Man has problem with authority figures.

32. Interview past or present authority figures. Find out what they are like as people.

Note

1. These assignments work best when there are clear, specific agreements between men in the group, all fully agreeing to the experiment.
2. These are a few challenges for a few situations. They can be used as they are or altered as needed to create more specific assignments for specific situations.

THINGS TO DO TOGETHER

Being composed of playful, adventurous creatures, a men's group that has been together for a while will naturally desire a change of pace. This is also part of the play I mentioned in Chapter 13. So your playful change of pace can replace regularly scheduled meetings or be an addition to your meetings. These creative adventures can take many forms, from inviting an individual with special skills or ideas to make a "guest appearance," to doing recreational activities that are significant to individual members.

Each man in your group has the opportunity to turn his new friends on to some activity or experience that he particularly enjoys and values. He has the pleasure of being the guide, and all the rest of your group benefits from a very personal tour.

Or there may be activities that just need to be done as a group and one member is willing to arrange and organize it. So it happens. The following are lists of possible alternative activities for group meetings. For convenience, they have been arranged by season and are meant to give you some direction in generating your own alternatives.

It is important that a consensus be reached among group members so that every member has input and feels that his wants are being heard.

Winter Activities   December–February

1. Attend the annual dog or cat show.
2. Build snowmen (or women).
3. Have a snowball fight.
4. Give each other presents at a holiday party.
5. Go cross-country skiing.
6. Start a contest among group members to see who gains the least weight between Christmas and New Year's.
7. Watch the Super Bowl together.
8. Rent a cabin in the woods for a weekend.
9. Take a hike in a wooded area.
10. Attend a free show at the planetarium.
11. Sing Christmas carols in public.
12. Attend a concert (symphony or rock 'n' roll).
13. Attend a sports event (major league or high school).
14. Make masks of yourselves and paint them.
15. Read the same book or article and discuss it in the group.

"Spring comes and the grass grows by itself."
—the Tao

Spring Activities   March–May

1. Members get together twice a week to exercise.
2. Go fly a kite.
3. Attend the circus.
4. Attend a film series at the university.
5. Take another hike and watch the plants budding.
6. Discuss the New Year's resolutions you made in January. How are you doing?
7. Go roller-skating outside together.
8. Attend a recital on a Sunday afternoon.
9. Go dancing together.
10. Plant a garden together.
11. Skip a meeting, and have each participant do an alternative, individual activity instead. Report what you each did. Be creative! Do something healing and rewarding for yourself.
12. Trace each other's bodies on large sheets of paper. Draw funny faces.
13. Have members of the group play blindman's buff.
14. Go out for dinner together.
15. Everyone take a day off from work and enjoy spring fever together!

Summer Activities   June–August

1. On a Sunday take a bike trip to a town at least twenty miles away.
2. Go to a flea market and buy some useful junk.
3. Have a squirt-gun fight outside.
4. Go horseback riding.
5. Rent a weekend cottage together.
6. Go skydiving.
7. Go bungee jumping together.
8. Hold group meetings outside.
9. Have a "Christmas in July" party. Sing holiday (winter) songs and exchange presents.
10. Form a team to play in a sports league. Baseball, volleyball, tennis are all sports with leagues. Or, just play for fun.
11. Attend sportscar, stock-car, or drag races.
12. Attend a summer concert in a park.
13. Go fishing.
14. Attend a county fair.
15. Have a picnic, play Frisbee, and go swimming at the local beach.

Autumn Activities   **September–November**

1. Attend an Oktoberfest celebration.
2. Write a letter to the local newspaper.
3. Make a list of three magazines that the group would like to subscribe to and purchase group subscriptions.
4. Pair up to take evening classes or training in something enjoyable at a trade school.
5. Once a month attend a movie together.
6. As a group, start a needed community resource or change some bureaucratic policy.
7. Attend a workshop or seminar together.
8. Go roller-skating or roller-discoing at a skating rink.
9. Take a day trip to a big city or small town.
10. Share a self-improvement weekend together, eating only healthy, natural foods, doing light exercise, and reading good books.
11. Take a trip to a large shopping mall. Form small sub-groups to pick out some new clothes for yourself.
12. Rent a gym to play volleyball or basketball.
13. Give each other lessons in things you do well, that men are interested in. Examples: piano playing, art, sports, cooking.
14. Pick apples together.
15. Take another hike. This is the best time of year. Combine it with a picnic.

If you still need an excuse or therapeutic justification to do some of this stuff, my prescription is that you are to think of it as a cure for that dread male malady of **workaholism,** and go play!

"MISSION" IN A MAN'S LIFE

A powerful possibility for your group is the inclusion of a rather sophisticated exercise to clarify each man's life "mission." I've observed and guided hundreds of men in their creation of a purpose in life that is bigger than the limits of their "personal" self. We call this realm the transpersonal. I've often shared the joy of men bursting into tears at the moment they make the leap from the separate "ego" self into the grander Self that includes all their fellow humans and the whole world.

The power of creating a transpersonal mission is incalculable. From the metaphysical truth that "thought creates reality," we know that whatever we think about and dwell on will eventually become manifest in our lives. Therefore, knowing what I'm creating makes it possible for me to ask my friends and colleagues, and especially fellow group members, to support my mission and help me focus in choosing stretches and goals in alignment with it.

Let's consider this idea of "mission" by using an archetypal metaphor, drawing on mythology. A mission is a warrior's quest. He carries out the mission of the sacred king (often his "inner king"). A warrior is a man with a focus/task/mission greater than himself. In the Middle Ages the knights took up the quest for the Holy Grail, sometimes barely knowing what it was, but believing in the process. It gave their lives incredible focus and purpose.

Sounds great, but many men would prefer it to be less filling. Today, there are too few warriors, not enough men of mission. But there are lots of soldiers looking for a father figure to guide their lives.

I consider the scarcity of "men of mission" to be a problem. The following analysis is one possible explanation as to why this void exists.

In the 1950s, *Time* magazine announced, "God is dead." What they meant was that for the first time in the history of our culture, people were no longer willing to accept the authority and dogma of organized Christian religions. In effect, people were saying, "We can figure it out for ourselves."

A positive effect of this view is that people were cutting free from external authority and reclaiming their own spiritual center as source.

The downside is that living in a capitalist culture without externally imposed Christian morality has given a green light to power-and-control addicts whose idea of accountability is to see what they can get away with. We have been observing the results of this on the six o'clock news for years. There was Watergate, the Iran-Contra controversy, and more recently the "October surprise" and S & L scandals.

The men responsible for those events do not seem to be acting in integrity. What they say and what they do are not the same thing. They are not men of mission. They do not hold themselves accountable and do not want anyone else to hold them accountable.

A solution to this problem is men living with a socially conscious mission, a worthwhile purpose in life. I believe that human behavior is intentional and we all are "on purpose," whether we know it or not.

The bad news is that most well-intentioned men, and women, do not have a clue as to what their personal life mission or purpose might be. They are living their lives according to unconscious reasons, often imparted to them by their parents, early church training, or media influence. On the evidence of their behavior, many people consider being a good consumer to be an important reason for living. "Shop till you drop," "Party till you puke," "He who dies with the most toys wins," are funny bumper stickers that people use to tell (albeit unconsciously) the world about their life purpose. They innocently flaunt the favorite addictions that cover their pain and feelings of meaninglessness.

The good news is that a healthy purpose, a conscious life mission, is quite accessible. If you want it, you can create it. The rest of this chapter is about doing that for yourself.

If your group has a "champion" for the cause of adding missions to your group, he likely will become process leader. He may want to use the following preparation and procedures for eliciting men's missions.

To the "mission process" champion: Get the support of the whole group. Make photocopies of this chapter and perhaps the next one. Hand them out and discuss the possibility of adding the clarification of life missions to your group process. Handle any resistance in the most accepting and loving way— the men are dealing with the essence of what their lives are about. This may take some weeks. When all the members of your group are ready to create their life missions, ask for a commitment of at least one full meeting. Prepare ahead to take the men through the process.

The mission process

1. So where do we start in finding our life mission? There is an old adage that our strength is in our "wound." For most of us growing up in what we now call "dysfunctional families," our wounds happened to us when we were young. Our wound could be anything, from abuse ("spanking" is now recognized as child abuse) to neglect (Dad was never there for his son). If we can access the little boy who lives in us, we can trust that he knows what his wound is and what he needs. Psychologist James Hillman says, "Every man's life mission is rooted in his little boy's deepest need." So let's find what our inner little boy most needs.

Materials: Notebook or 3 x 5 cards and a pen for each man.

Action: It works well to guide your group through an imaginary trip we call a visualization. Begin by inviting them to get into a comfortable position, either sitting or lying down, and to close their eyes. To prevent their falling asleep, suggest that they keep one arm up and resting on the elbow, which will fall and awaken them if they nod off.

Now comes the relaxation part. Use your imagination to create a word-picture of a quiet, peaceful scene, perhaps a natural setting such as an island or forest. Continue to invite them to *"relax"* and *"relax a little deeper."* You are actually taking them into a light trance, and by now they probably trust you enough to go with you. (Five to ten minutes)

Once they are relaxed, invite them to see a small boy off in the distance, and as he comes closer, suggest that they recognize him as themselves when very young. Slowly, instruct them to reach out to the boy, take him in their arms, and ask him what he needs most. They listen and remember what he says.

Then slowly bring them back up, reversing whatever path you took them on to get them deeply relaxed. Once they are back to full, waking consciousness, instruct them to write down their little boy's deepest need.

2. This step invites men to create a "vision" of a possibility in the world. Say: *"Now, again close your eyes, relax* (pause), *and from what you wrote down as your little boy's deepest need,* **imagine** *if the whole world had that* (pause), *if everyone on the planet had what your little boy needs, what would it look like* (pause), *feel like* (pause), *sound like* (pause), *be like? See it, feel it* (pause). *How would the world be different* (pause)? *That's your* **vision.** *Write it down."* Repeat the instruction if necessary. Wait until every man is finished.

3. This step enables men to focus on their own action in making the vision happen. Say: *"Now, again close your eyes, relax, and see yourself some-how making your vision happen* (pause). *How are you doing it* (pause)? *It may be in your current work situation, or some other way* (pause). *How are you doing it? Write it down; that is your* **action.**" Repeat if necessary. Go on until all have written enough.

4. The next step—an important one—is combining the vision and the action. *"Now, combine your* **vision** *with your* **action** *into your mission. Write a mission statement, which is your vision of a possible world and how you are making it happen. Do the best you can, write something, we will be doing some clarifying soon."* (Wait until most have completed writing something.)

5. Now we move into discussion. Ask two men, in turn, to present their newly created "mission." Invite the group to give feedback to each man, while he just **listens** (no dialogue). **"Is this a mission, why or why not?"** is the basic question the group members should ask themselves in framing their feedback to the man who stated the mission. *"Is this a combination of his vision and action?"* You may need to repeat this several times. Be patient and let the men do the work. The learning here is in the **feedback process**, the men are **learning by creating it themselves** with each other's support, not by being told. (Continue until both are complete.) Thank them.

Note: It may be a slow process at this point. Give the men some reassurance that this may be a very new and complex experience. Encourage them to be patient with themselves in going through it.

6. At this point, give some educational information on vision, action, mission, and goals. (See "Mission" page at the end of this chapter, make copies ahead for each man.) Use discussion as necessary.

Say: *"Now, using this new information, take some time to rewrite your mission if necessary."* (until most have finished writing) *"Now write two goals that are supporting your mission."* (until most have finished writing)

7. Once again, ask for two men to present his **mission** and his **goals** to check accuracy and alignment. Ask for feedback from group. *"Is that a mission as we have come to understand it and are his goals in alignment?"* (until both have presented)

8. Instruct: *"Now rewrite it if necessary into a final mission statement.*

My life mission is _____ *."*
(until most are complete)

9. As a group, rework and clarify each man's mission. Each man presents his mission in its present form. The group may refer to his action and goals in inviting him to hone and refine his mission. The group will sense the man's passion and energy when he gets his right mission. It just **feels** right. Congratulations!

10. Discuss, and make some decisions about how you are going to continue to support each other's missions. For example: you could make mission statements a regular ongoing part of your group, by including them every meeting during Rounds. They also might bring up some great material for stretches. See the next chapter for ways to take your missions out into the world. Enjoy.

> **"I don't know what your destiny will be, but one thing I do know: The only ones among you who will be really happy are those who have sought and found how to serve."**
> **—Albert Schweitzer**

"Mission"

Little boy's deepest needs
Vision = possibility
Action = how I'm making it happen
Mission = Vision + Action
Goals = measurable steps along the way

Definition and distinctions

Your **"vision"** is what you imagine as possible if your "little boy's" need were fulfilled for everyone on the entire planet. It is your creation of a new world using your ability to visualize and feel.

Your **"action"** is how you are making your vision happen. It may be in your current work situation or in an avocation. It is what you do every day in big and small ways to create your vision.

Your **"mission"** is your vision plus your action. It is your quest, your dream, your passion, what your life is about. It is so big, so important, that your mission may never be completed in your lifetime. And it includes the "how"—your action, what you do.

Your **"goals"** are those specific, measurable, and timely achievements in support of your mission. They are tangible. They are doable. And the accomplishment of them gets you closer in some way to realizing your mission.

Some process suggestions

1. If a man has **"I-centered"** mission: use the metaphor of "A mission is like a **river** flowing out of us, not like a **lake** which is self-contained." Look for the **flow.**

2. If a man can't get the difference between **mission** and **goals:** use the metaphor of mission being a direction, such as **west.** To get west from New York I go to Chicago, Denver, San Francisco, Hawaii, Hong Kong, etc. The achievable stops along the way are like goals, and we may never totally achieve our mission. Richard Bach in his book, *Illusions,* says, "Here is a test to find whether your mission on earth is finished: If you're alive, it isn't."

3. Some **examples** of missions: A businessman: "I create love in the world through empowering people to realize their dreams." An artist: "I create beauty through art." A man doing men's work: "I create a safe planet through empowering men." A physician: "I create a healthy world through awareness." A journalist: "I heal the world through communication." A family therapist: "I create harmony by building bridges between people."

MEN TAKING ACTION IN THE WORLD

Men's work, recovery, and empowerment for what? We can empower and initiate men. The highest-level question remains—so what?

Men's work refers to the process of honorable, initiated men actively empowering and initiating men. Recovery can be viewed as the long process of initiation. Mature masculinity, the fully initiated man, is an ideal to strive for. The initiated man does what is necessary to meet his responsibilities as a man.

A men's support group is a great start. It can contain recovery. Healing. It can be a place to share failures and successes in the initiation process. A man who is getting healthier and stronger will want to be involved in some larger way, channeling his energy into something beyond himself. He may start close to home with his family, then move out into the community and the world. He becomes a man of mission. (See Chapter 20.)

In 1984, my mission unfolded as *"I create a safe planet through empowering men."* I wanted the bombs off our planet, and I knew I would need help. I formed a **group of men** and we took action. We co-created the New Warrior Training, with a group mission to *empower men to missions of service*. I know that the power of a **group of men** with aligned missions can be awesome.

"Our" planet: It is being said more often now, and I hope you have heard it before: the survival of our planet is in the hands of our generation. I honor Australian physician Helen Caldicott for her courage to say the things that no one wanted to hear. Ten years ago she was educating us about the unthinkable medical consequences of nuclear war. More recently she has been focusing on the environmental catastrophe in progress. We must find the courage to hear, without going numb, when she and others suggest that without significant planetary action we have ten years left.

There is a school of thought among deep ecologists that if we truly face the world's environmental situation, it will bring up grief around our mortality. So, as isolated individuals, we may tend to feel overwhelmed and go into addictions or denial. Doing the inevitable grief work in a supportive men's group can take us beyond the despair. To carry the great weight of the responsibilities we face, we need the support and stimulation of other men.

Men as warriors have always protected their women and children. Today, "Mother Earth" is in mortal danger, with all her children at risk. That includes you and me and our children. We must bond together with men if we hope to feel empowered enough to address the tasks facing us.

Lionel Tiger, in his book, *Men In Groups,* says that in human evolution men tended to bond together in groups to face crises. The nature of masculinity is for men in groups to empower each other to do what they need to do to ensure the survival of the community. It is imperative that we draw on this evolutionary heritage and bond together globally to respond to our common planetary problems.

I'm not suggesting that men turn aside from our process or ritual groups, or from dancing, drumming, joyful poetry, or myth. These are expressions of male power and magnificence that carry over into the action needed to bring safety, justice, and peace to their world.

I also want you to know there is hope. We have made some gains. The whales are safer, the elephant slaughter has been dramatically reduced, and the rain forests are in less danger of total devastation. And we have the technology to control the global population explosion. Take a humble little bow and let's get back to work.

Stewardship: This term means caring for our home, city, planet. Men have long had a role in stewarding and protecting women and children. The following are some directions you and/or your group can use to take action in stewarding our planet.

> "If one is to do good one must do it in the minute particulars. General good is the plea of the hypocrite, the flatterer, and the scoundrel."
>
> —William Blake

Some organizations devoted to

Environment: Greenpeace, Rainforest Action Network, Sierra Club, Environmental Defense Fund, Friends of the Earth, Earthstewards Network

Communication: Better World Society

Peace and justice: Beyond War, Amnesty International, American Friends Service Committee, Planetary Citizens

Inner cities: Urban League, NAACP, Junior Achievement

Working with young people: Boy Scouts, Big Brothers, 4-H Clubs, Peacechild Foundation

Politics: Local, state, national, and global affairs are our business. As we come to know our own power we can stop idealizing our leaders and assuming that they know what they are doing or that they have our best interests in mind. Our responsibility is to use our male warrior energy to demand their integrity and hold them accountable for behaving according to their word. Our lives, our children's lives, and the planet depend on our being vigilant watchdogs of our leaders' stewardship.

If you don't want to get involved with existing organizations, your group might develop a local project: plant trees, highway clean-up, visit men in prison, feed homeless people, recycle, reuse, cut down on consumables. To get started on something soon, I have a recommendation. David Gershon, coauthor with his wife, Gail Straub, of *Empowerment: The Art of Creating Your Life As You Want It*, has predesigned a step-by-step project any group can adapt and use. You become, for six months, an "Ecoteam" supporting each other's families in healing our planet. Write for information to: Global Action Plans for the Earth, 84 Yerry Hill Rd., Woodstock, NY 12498.

Group mission: A group mission is a way for your whole group to take another step in its development. It can be a task you decide to take on as a group.

Many of the ideas and words contained in this chapter were drawn directly from the audiotape, "Dancing the Four Quarters: Masculine Leadership in the 1990s," by Robert Moore and Forrest Craver, and are used with their permission.

PART FOUR
SITUATIONS AND DYNAMICS IN YOUR GROUP

"When you do meet with men, then meet with men. Don't have a woman near the meeting space, no matter how much positive regard or relatedness she shares with you. Men's-lodge space is a private, *sacred space*. Since the dawn of time men in every culture have met alone and in secret to approach their gods and find their collective magic. Every little boy knows this instinctively—'No Girlz Allowed.' "

— Aaron R. Kipnis, Ph.D., *Knights Without Armor*

HANDLING PROBLEMS IN GROUPS

The following problems are among the most common and challenging developments that can hinder your group. And, worse, they could lead to a premature end to the group or be harmful to individuals. These "problems" sometimes involve the full group, sometimes an individual member.

It is **your** responsibility as a group member to get what you want from your group. This may mean speaking up and confronting the problem situation when you notice it.

Group problems

The summer slump: The lazy season is a reality not to be ignored. Having observed a lot of groups over nearly two decades, I've noticed that they often break up over summer. Men think the others are losing interest, whereas it is just lazy vacation time. So be aware and plan ahead. In spring discuss the upcoming summer and make a group decision. Maybe you will decide to keep meeting through summer or take July, August, or both off. If you take time off, be sure to set an exact date to regroup.

The one-note group: One important way men learn and grow is by taking risks, by trying something new and unfamiliar. When a group falls into the pattern of taking little or no risk in its meetings, the members soon find they are not getting much.

Such a one-note group usually develops this way: One or two men lead off with a particular type of learning experience. They are successful, and the men responsible for planning the next group use a similar approach. After a while, the group starts to go stale. Men come to each meeting knowing what to expect. A safe learning style has been developed, but it becomes less and less effective because the elements of variety and risk are gone.

This is not to say that a group cannot repeat a successful learning experience. Sometimes a group might even make an agreement to stay with a certain process for a number of weeks. Repetition can work, as long as the group is then willing to take the risk of trying something else at the end of a sequence.

A one-note group is a dangerous development, but it is not difficult to avoid. Each member, in planning for a meeting, can be aware of the kinds of learning experiences recently used by the group and choose an approach that will not be repetitious.

The stuck-in-Rounds trap: This is a common variation of the "one-note group." In this group the opening, Rounds, slowly gets longer and longer until it takes up the entire time together. If your group has slipped into this pattern, talk about it and take corrective action. (See Chapter 8 on Rounds.)

The bull session: This is a low-risk group that uses theoretical discussion almost exclusively. There is nothing wrong with a good discussion, but we men need to get beyond the "bull." When this is the primary learning style, the members soon begin to feel "nothing is happening." They start thinking, "We're not getting much out of this group."

Men traditionally have used intellectualization as a hedge against expressing feelings we were taught to ignore. Staying at the feeling level in a group is a significant challenge. In terms of experiencing personal authenticity and real closeness, it is essential. (See Chapter 9 on feelings.)

To avoid this pitfall, the man who is responsible for planning the next meeting will consider whether the group has had too much of the discussion approach, and whether more focus on feelings or a commitment to action might be more useful for the meeting.

The party-time group: Members of this happy group enjoy each other so much that they start each meeting twenty minutes late because they hate to break up their conversations. Their ten-minute breaks become half-hour occasions to talk about last week's football game, U.S. foreign policy, vacation plans, or whatever. A major part of each meeting may be a discussion about what refreshments could be provided for the next meeting, and the meeting finishes a bit early in order to appreciate more fully the culinary delights that are the product of the last meeting's negotiations.

This sort of avoidance behavior is a serious issue. If a few attempts do not shake the pattern, it must be confronted squarely. This might happen in an evaluation meeting, or through any man willing to risk challenging what is going on. If you recognize that your group falls into this pattern, remind the others of their purpose for having a group. That is usually enough to get the group back on track.

Individual member problems

The dominating member: This is the man who takes more than his share of the group's attention, talks too much, asks too many questions, or dominates the topics being discussed. He is usually a constructive participant who overdoes it. But he defeats the purpose of the group, which is meant to give all the men the chance to be highly involved.

The best way to avoid this problem is for each man to monitor his own participation. Sometimes this means not speaking when you have something to say, in order to let others have a little more time to think and speak. Activities can also be structured to reduce domination by one or two members. For example, use subgroups and give each man the focus for a set period of time.

If you are in a group with a dominating member, it is your responsibility to intervene. This can be done at the evaluation session or by a friendly comment such as, "Jerry, I've found your ideas really interesting, and I'd like to hear more from the others," or some such comment. If other men support this feedback, a dominating member will likely get the message and he may even be offered an opportunity to deal with his need to showboat, control, or be the center of attention.

The imposing member: This man appears certain that his ideas and suggestions are obviously correct or the best available. The words and tone convey the message: "Here's the answer, this is the way it's done, obviously, I'm right." This behavior tends to intimidate the rest of the group because the members do not want their comments to be judged by someone who is convinced of his own power and brilliance. This is a big one for men, because we were taught to have the solution and put it out strongly.

Again, each group member must be alert to avoid this behavior in himself. Since it usually is easier to spot a behavior in someone else than in oneself, other group members may have to point this out to an imposing member by saying, "I feel judged whenever you react to my ideas. It seems as though you're always trying to get me to agree with you. Is that right? If it is, it makes me feel very uncomfortable." Or, "That comment seems like a solution and we've agreed to not provide solutions without permission." Try whatever seems appropriate. But take care not to impose an equally rigid judgment on an imposing member.

Ernie comes to the realization that he's been monopolizing the group's time over the last few sessions.

The quiet member: Sometimes a man will seem to get lost in the group. He shows up every week, but rarely says more than his Rounds check-in and closing comment. He may be draining energy from the group, who feel a need to take care of him.

Getting the concern open to the group usually works to relieve the excessive caretaking and invites him in to play. A direct, heartfelt comment will often open the door. For example: "Tom, I've noticed that you don't talk up very much in group and I'm concerned."

The roadblock member: Each group member is responsible for speaking up, disagreeing when it is appropriate, and making his needs known. However, there are times when it is more appropriate for a member, having expressed dissent on an issue, to go along with the group to prevent it from getting totally bogged down. The man who cannot seem to make this concession is Mr. Roadblock.

There are times, especially when moral issues are involved, when it is courageous to say no to a group and halt its progress. In support groups, however, a consistent roadblocker may be a man who is in the wrong group or who has an emotional need to get his own way. The group will help both itself and him by refusing to go along with this behavior pattern. Suggestions such as, "I see us going around in circles now, so how about going along with the group on this one and seeing how it works out?" will usually do the trick. If not, the roadblocking can be discussed and confronted more fully at an evaluation meeting.

The scapegoat member: Sometimes a support group will blame group problems on a particular man. The process is called scapegoating and can be very detrimental. Scapegoating is a process that family counselors have known about for a long time. It often happens when parents direct hostility meant for each other onto one of the children.

In your group, scapegoating can be harmful in several ways to both the group and the man who is singled out. A great deal of hostility may be directed toward one man, and it is often more than he can handle. The scapegoat is often a man who has broken the informal rules or norms of the group. (For instance, in a group where intellectual, logical discussions are emphasized, a man who talks about feelings may be picked on as a scapegoat, or vice-versa.) The treatment given to such a man is unjust and often cruel. And too often the scapegoat may be a particularly narcissistic man who honestly does not know what he is doing that is making others angry.

Yet another government program that's gone too far.

Scapegoating is a group problem because it lets the rest of the group off the hook. It allows them to shirk responsibility for problems, avoid feelings, and put the blame on something outside themselves. Scapegoating inhibits solving problems creatively because it limits the focus of men's thoughts and attentions. Furthermore, scapegoating can give the group a common but negative identity, as members unite in freezing their viewpoints on a single common issue, that of blaming someone else for their problems.

As an observant member you can help the group be aware of its behavior. Often you can do this by rephrasing the accusation in more general terms and addressing it as a problem of the group. Such a problem is rarely an individual man's doing, and is usually caused by some shortcoming in the way the group operates. Help your group see how the scapegoat is useful to the group in that role, and how they might address the issues so a scapegoat is not needed.

It is also possible for a group to scapegoat an issue or a situation. Men may unite in blaming the "women" or the "government" for their dissatisfaction and lack of feeling successful. This kind of scapegoating is as bad for a group as scapegoating an individual.

Summary of skills for handling disruptive members of the group

1. Give straight, clear, descriptive feedback—tell the man how you are feeling at that moment and what specific behavior of his brought about that feeling.
2. Propose alternatives—tell the disruptive member that you think he is getting in the way of the group's process and that he probably has valid but different priorities. Ask him what he would rather do at this time.

LEAVING THE GROUP

Sometime in the future, for any one of a variety of reasons, someone will find it necessary to leave the group. This is a natural, understandable, and usually necessary step to take. It means that he no longer needs the group because he has grown and changed, or he is moving to New Zealand. There can be a million good reasons. Fortunately, if your group followed this manual from the outset, each of you agreed in the first meeting to say good-bye when it came time to leave. Honoring that agreement will make this separation a lot easier.

Separation is often difficult for us, so there is a good possibility that powerful, conflicting feelings will come up for the man leaving the group. Sadness, perhaps happiness or guilt, sometimes anger, and even fear are the emotions a man may feel when leaving a group of men he is close to.

The other men may be having similar feelings about his leaving the group. This is also natural and expected. They may fantasize about why he is leaving if they are not told the reasons—especially if he just decides not to come anymore and simply doesn't show up. Separation pushes all our buttons and needs to be handled as openly and clearly as possible.

I strongly suggest that when a man leaves the group, he tell the group of his decision and then share his feelings and reasons in person. It will also be helpful to tie up any loose ends that exist between him and other members. Sometimes there is so much healing in this process that he chooses to stay with the group.

"Good-bye" rituals: The man leaving can get a sense of completion for himself and for the group with the following exit ritual. He gives each man direct feedback on how he feels about him. Then, **after he has given each member his feedback**, each man gives him **one** piece of feedback about him. Below are simplistic examples of how this exercise might sound:

Example: Jim is leaving the group.

Jim: "Roy, I'm going to miss your weird sense of humor."
Roy: "Jim, I see you as a very charismatic person."

Jim: "Tom, I think you are a very sensitive man."
Tom: "Jim, I'm going to miss your jokes; you make me smile."

Jim: "Bob, I still feel angry toward you."
Bob: "Jim, sometimes I think you were sarcastic to me."

Jim: "Jack, sometimes I felt you being impatient with me."
Jack: "Jim, I feel afraid sometimes when you get quiet."

Jim: "Carl, I feel very comfortable with you."

Carl: "I would like to get together with you sometime soon, because I enjoy your company."

An alternative and simpler, yet useful way of structuring a good-bye ritual is to have each man give one positive gift of feedback and one "bon voyage" good wish to the man leaving.

"Good-bye form": As a way of guiding your group consciously through the often emotionally charged separation process, on the next page in this manual is a "Good-bye form." It asks questions the man leaving might want to consider before leaving. It may help him clarify what he needs to say to the group to feel complete before he leaves.

Good-bye form

Name _____ Date _____

This form is to assist you in the separation from your group. It is intended as a guide in focusing your awareness on your feelings and beliefs about leaving the group at this time.

1. What is your reason(s) for leaving the group?

2. What are your feelings about leaving?

3. What have you accomplished in this group?

4. What would you like to see change in this group?

5. Is there any "unfinished business" that needs to be completed with the group or with individual men before you leave?

6. Is there anything you need from the group, or want to give before you leave?

7. Are there any specific communications you need to make with anyone in the group before you leave?

A Circle of Men: The Official Manual for Men's Support Groups © 1992 Bill Kauth

I know of one men's group I organized here in the Milwaukee area that ran for over ten years, and by that time there was only one original member. That group's longevity was due to its being able to add new members successfully.

A concern that will arise eventually in your men's support group is how and when to add new members. Any group will lose members over time, for all sorts of valid reasons. There will be men who no longer need the group, men who want to spend more time with their kids, or men who are moving far away.

This is a significant change because when the circle gets too small, it can become difficult to maintain the level of energy and communication that a group requires. This can lead to apathy and disenchantment. Let's consider some factors about adding new members.

Open and closed groups

A group that allows new members to join at any time is called an open group. Open groups can provide immediate support to men in crisis. However, a group that constantly has new members will have a difficult time generating a group identity and promoting trust between members.

A group that does not admit new members is called a closed group. Both have their advantages and uses. Closed groups can provide a more complete level of trust.

The appropriate men's support group compromise is a closely held semi-open group that allows a limited number of new members into the group at certain times, usually to fill the spot of a man who has left. Frequently these groups will set a minimum number of participants and when the group goes below that minimum, it will bring in new men to fill those places. A support group works best with nine members. I suggest seven as a minimum.

Finding new members

A useful rule of thumb is that the better known a man is to the current group members, the more easily he will be integrated into the group. So the simplest and best way to find new members is for the current members to consider their friends or acquaintances. Inviting the new man to a group social gathering before he is actually invited into the group is a way for all involved to check each other out without any commitment up front. If your group socializes together you probably know some of your friends' friends already.

Another method is to advertise (see Chapter 4) for new members. This is less safe because there is little personal contact before the new man comes in contact with the group. It probably will be important to do some screening.

MEN'S GROUP WIVES
BENEFIT RUMMAGE SALE

USED PEDESTALS

SHORT LEASHES

Another method that has had success is to contact organizations composed of individuals like yourselves. A contact person at the organization can assist in screening men for your group and you will have a greater guarantee of having common interests. This allows for greater diversity than if you simply work through friends.

The important idea to keep in mind is that this need for new members is a natural phase that all groups go through. It is healthy and shows that your group is helping men change. Bringing in new men can be an exciting new phase for a group and can be a positive experience in critically examining the strengths, goals, and needs of the group and its members. Remember also that when new members join the group, it is once again a "new" group and needs to work through some of the earlier phases of group development.

Entering the group

The actual incorporation of a new member into your group is challenging new business. It is like bringing a new member into your family. It is very important to create a ritual introduction to acquaint a new member and the group with one another. For example, each member could present a five-minute life history and then a few minutes on what has happened in the group and what these events have meant in their lives. The new member then might share an overview of his life and include his intentions and commitment to the group. If each man shares his feelings, both historical ones and his feelings in the moment, the bonding will proceed more rapidly.

Any activity that clearly acknowledges the entry of the new member will work. And the more feelings, statements of intention, and shared background, the better.

Physical touch is a delicate subject in men's groups. Most of us have been taught not to touch each other in any affectionate way. We generally figured out rough and tough alternatives like football, wrestling, and good-natured jostling—all of which work fine and feel appropriately masculine.

The problem is that they don't work so well in groups. Unfortunately, a step-over toehold or good, solid cross-body block just doesn't get it when a man is feeling sad and may need a more gentle, supportive touch.

So it's a wonderful stretch for us men to learn and make okay for ourselves the softer types of touch. There are many times in and out of group when these touches are totally appropriate.

Hugs: Man-to-man hugs sure are getting more popular than they were ten or fifteen years ago, and I think it's great. I've been to many social gatherings of friends lately where the men hug each other and shake hands with the women. We seem to have broken free of a major taboo of the old culture. However, we are still in transition, so I've developed some guidelines that may be useful.

1. Talk about hugging: In your group it may be very useful just to talk about hugging at one of your early meetings. Give every man an opportunity to share his feelings about hugging. This will probably lead to discussion about physical touch with Dad, and fear of homosexuality, hostile locker-room talk, etc. This is valuable stuff to be sharing, as it frees us to let our deprivations and fears be known. It helps men learn that affection and intimacy have very little to do with sexuality (a major confusion for most of us).

2. "Ritual hugs": Some groups use hugs as a greeting and good-bye "ritual" (see Chapter 26). It is a great alternative to shaking hands. It provides a lot of physical closeness with full group support and a wonderful opportunity to practice. As you get better at hugging, you may notice that you are patting each other on the back a lot less.

3. Permission: My experience is that it takes different men different time to get used to and comfortable with hugging other men. Permission not to hug is important. Peer-pressure-forced hugging may be worse than no hugs at all. Sometimes it may be important for a man very uncomfortable with hugs to request all members of his group to ask his permission before they hug. The group must respect this request and lovingly accept a handshake if that is all that is available for now.

4. Teaching: Sometimes one man who is more comfortable with hugs can very gently invite another man to relax and learn to hug him. I clearly remember when a man did that for me. We were in a situation in which my role meant I was to be supportive of him, and as I was hugging him good-bye, Mark lovingly said, "Dammit, Bill, relax and just be with me." I did, and it became a wonderful gift he gave to me, and I have gently passed it on to hundreds of other men over the years.

Supportive touch: There may be times in your group when the feelings of one or more men will be openly expressed. When grief in the form of tears or when crying or sobbing happens, there is often confusion about whether or not to touch the man as a way of supporting his process. There are obviously no hard rules here. However, I do want to suggest some guidelines:

1. Trust your intuition: If it "feels" right, make the physical contact with the man who seems to need it. This is "knowing" the difference between being supportive and rescuing him.

2. Trust him to know what he needs: Ultimately it is up to the man who is experiencing the feeling to accept or not to accept the offered touch. He will know if he needs support or can go through the experience with your simply being in the room beside him.

3. Type of physical contact: The situation may call for a simple hand on his shoulder or a full hug in which he can experience the grief more completely. The supportive touch can be given spontaneously, perhaps by men sitting near the man working. The hug will be more invitational. Example: *"Do you want to be held while you are going through this feeling?"*

4. Touch vs. patting: This has to do with how to touch. Sometimes men tend to rub, pat, or stroke the man in an attempt to be supportive. Unfortunately, this can sometimes be distracting to the emotional work he is doing. I suggest just placing your hand on his back or shoulder, to let him know quietly you are there and you care.

The notion of men touching is emotionally loaded because it often takes us to an awareness of our father hunger. As John Lee states in his heartfelt book, *At My Father's Wedding,* "When we hold out our hands to another man or take him in our arms to be held, he will most likely feel the father's hands he never held reaching through time and space." Your group is a safe place to do your work. Ask for what you need.

RITUAL IN MEN'S GROUPS

"If it works use it" is often a rule of thumb in the evolution of men's groups. Ritual is one of those strange and sometimes misunderstood processes that seem to work. I see ritual all the time in groups and think it would be useful for you to know about it.

What is ritual? The briefest definition I've heard is, **"Ritual is anything that worked once and got repeated."** Our lives are full of rituals that we do day in and day out. Some are functional, but we would be hard pressed, if asked, to say why we do others.

A more formal definition: Ritual is any repetitive practice or procedure done as a rite. Rites are ceremonial, formal acts, or procedures prescribed by custom. Most of what we do every day is prescribed by, and an enactment of, the mythology of some social, religious, or family custom. Shopping is rooted in the myth of consumerism. What time we get up, brush our teeth, have coffee in the morning, what (or whether) we eat at breakfast, pray before the meal, read the paper, hug (or not) the kids, kiss (or not) our wife good-bye, etc.—all serve, or once served, some function based on belief/mythology.

Ritual is everywhere. One that we, as men, will all be aware of is the social rite of courtship. We know about the carefully prescribed dating steps and procedures we have been dealing with since we were in high school. Warren Farrell in his 1986 book, *Why Men Are the Way They Are*, talks about the unspoken ritualized process of taking sexual initiatives with women. He points out that we can expect to "risk rejection about 150 times between eye contact and sexual contact." Why we men take all the risks is rooted in myths about men and women. Your group may want to talk about that sometime. Meanwhile, let's consider two types of rituals.

Social rituals: They are, as suggested by the examples above, functional. There is something comforting about everyday rituals. They do not have to be thought about or recreated each time. There is a sense of belonging built into some social rituals, a feeling of identification with the culture, religion, or family from which the ritual evolved. Other social rituals form a code of behavior that, although unspoken, provides safety for people who are strangers to each other.

Ceremonial rituals: Formal ritual serves as a sort of transformer for powerful archetypal energy. This is the energy of transformation, of changing consciousness from one state of being to another. The most obvious in our men's work is the transition from boyhood to manhood. Historically, most groups or tribes of people had awareness of such a process and honored it through some ritual, a rite of passage.

The ceremony (ritual) was a safe space in which the transformation could happen. I think it is important to note for my fellow linear-thinking men that I'm talking about intuitive process here. We "know" it and honor it, whether it makes logical sense or not.

The idea of ritual as a transformational container is rooted in C. G. Jung's concept of the two-million-year-old man who lives in all of us. It is the energy we share just by being human males. It is accessible to us through our genetic coding and/or our connection to the "collective unconscious." Jungian analyst Robert Moore has suggested that the archetypal (more on archetypes in Chapter 30) energy is so powerful that to attempt to access it without going through the ritual transformer would be like plugging a toaster directly into a nuclear power plant. So let us use this energy with awareness and all due respect.

Purpose of rituals in men's groups

We use ceremonial ritual to bring us together, with shared intention and focus. To create mutually the safety necessary for change to happen, to enact a certain mythology and sometimes create an altered state of consciousness. You may notice that rituals are connected with one or more of our senses, which grounds them in our physical reality. Some examples:

1. Opening Rounds: A repetitive process that offers consistency, group focus, and bonding. (as noted in Chapter 8)

2. Smudging: The use of smudge sticks (sage and cedar bound together) burned in a symbolic cleansing. It is a ritual washing away the cares of the day, the negative energies. This is borrowed rather directly from our Native American brothers. It is excellent non-linear thought preparation for being together.

3. Chanting: The blending of voices in a sound (om, aum, ram), a phrase, or a song (we found doing the old hymn "Amen" with an emphasis on the "men" part of it is great fun in men's groups). This brings the energies of the men together. Chanting, by the nature of the vibrations it creates, can also alter consciousness. There is an inner peacefulness that often accompanies the process of vibrating in harmony with others.

4. Spirit chair: A symbolic honoring and modeling of men who live in our awareness. In the New Warrior groups we sometimes bring in the "spirit" of a **Warrior**. He is a (now dead) man deeply committed to something worthwhile, a man whom we admire. In my own group of business executives we bring in a **King** spirit. He then sits with us (sometimes in a separate "empty" chair) during the meeting as a **presence we can emulate**. We gratefully send him back when we are done. The "bringing the spirit in" part of the ritual involves standing in a close circle with our right hands in the air and starting with a loud sound that becomes soft as we bring our hands down together in the middle of the group, implying that he is here with us now.

The "sending him back" ritual is the reverse. Hands down in middle, soft sound building and exploding loudly as we throw our hands skyward, implying that he has gone back. It's a great way to end each meeting. (Some examples of men whose "spirits" we have invited to sit with us: Gandhi, Abraham Lincoln, John Lennon, Crazy Horse, and Martin Luther King, Jr.)

5. Drumming: It seems that many groups across North America are using the ancient ritual of drumming to create the desired sacred space in which to do their work. Drumming can be used to open the group, close it, or both. The vibrations of this ritual are so powerful that you and your group might want to invest the time in making your own drums, or the money to buy some fine-quality drums. You might also seek out a man to teach you some drumming techniques.

Please appreciate the ancient power of drumming.

6. Talking stick: The stick itself, often decorated with feathers and fur, is a ritual object with specific meaning. Borrowed from our Native American brothers, the talking stick represents respecting a man speaking from his heart. All listen to the man holding the stick. Sometimes a man takes the stick to be sure he is heard, other times it is passed ceremonially around the circle.

7. Closing ritual: This could be gathering the group in a circle arm in arm, chanting, hugging, or reading a passage from which everyone takes inspiration. Whatever your group creates as its closing ritual, it is repeated consistently and means the end of that meeting.

8. Make up your own: Once you get a sense of needing a ritual for a specific purpose, make a suggestion about what might work or, better yet, ask your group for ideas about a ritual to serve the purpose. When the group is in consensus, try it out. If it works once, it may work again. However rituals evolve, try innovations that just might work even better.

"Instead of copying all of the time, I like to change the meaning once in a while to keep it interesting."

Ritual men's groups: Some groups exist with mythology as their primary focus. These are known as "ritual groups" and they take on the challenge of creating their own spiritual experiences. As your group matures, you may want to do more transformational ritual processes. If your group is ready and/or interested, I recommend Wayne Liebman's book, *Tending the Fire*.

THE STAGES OF GROUP DEVELOPMENT

It has been shown by research and experience that all groups go through certain specific stages of group development. It may be useful for your group members to understand these stages of development, **no matter who is in your group**. While there are a variety of theories about how many stages there are and how they are named, I think the brevity and alliteration of these make them memorable and therefore useful:

1. Groping stage: This is the first stage of development, where members are confused about their roles in the group and what exactly it is all about. At this stage, the group is really a bunch of individuals in the same room at the same time. **Membership issues are up.**

2. Griping stage: This is a period of discouragement, discomfort, conflict, and frustration. Group members have difficulty adjusting to the place (roles) in the group that each man has found for himself. **Control issues are up**.

3. Grasping stage: Efforts are made toward developing group harmony and avoiding conflicts. (They may still exist.) Members begin to be more comfortable with each other. **Affection issues are up**.

4. Grouping stage: Group members develop a sense of purpose and a sense of commitment to the group and begin to do some more risky "men's work" together. **Ongoing affection issues are up**.

This "stages" theory may be useful to your group for an occasional where-are-we-now evaluation. It may take weeks, months, or longer to get to the grouping stage, and your group may return at times to an earlier stage, but each time it will pass through the stage more effectively.

The following is a useful clarification on the stages that groups go through from an individual member's perspective. Will Schutz identified these issues in a book over twenty years ago.

The three significant interpersonal issues in groups

1. Membership (significance). This is an inclusion-exclusion issue. "Am I in or out?" This is an issue in virtually all relationships and goes back to how we were accepted into the world as infants. In groups, different men confront this issue at different times. Techniques for inclusion include: rounds, doing communication exercises in pairs, inviting the more quiet men in, and using structured learning experiences when men are ready to face the issues head-on.

2. Control (competence). This is the classic men's issue of power, authority, and competition. "How much influence do I have here?" Everyone wants to be in control to some degree. In different groups men control in different ways.

The obvious technique for getting beyond the control issue is to make clear that the group belongs to the members. Remind each other that "we are in control of what happens in our group, and we are here to be of service to each other in doing our men's work." Men will experience their own power at different points in the evolution of the group.

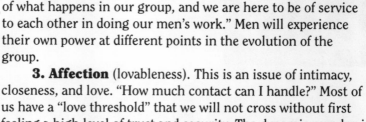

3. Affection (lovableness). This is an issue of intimacy, closeness, and love. "How much contact can I handle?" Most of us have a "love threshold" that we will not cross without first feeling a high level of trust and security. The dynamic paradox is that in these groups, the trust we are consistently building encourages men gradually to cross their love threshold. This in turn constantly brings up new fears around being known, parental issues, women, homophobia, anger, etc. Please recall (Chapter 12) that it is through the process of dealing with these conflicts that deeper trust and friendship grow. As the members of a group sort out their feelings toward one another, subgroups will evolve. This is extremely important to the continued growth and development of the group as a whole.

Note: If you know where your group is, you can speed up the process of getting to someplace you want to go by increasing the awareness of each stage of its development.

GROUP DYNAMICS

The word "dynamic" connotes energy—and change. This chapter is on "group dynamics," because the roles in a group are highly changeable and flexible. Very few group members play only one role. Each man usually acts out a combination of roles in the group because he has a number of goals he is reaching for. Some of these roles we may be aware of, some we may not. These next pages will help you to recognize and discuss some of the things that are taking place in your group.

There are two distinct levels of group interaction and communication: content and process.

Content is **what** the group or individual men are talking about. The subject matter, the topics, and feelings discussed are the content.

Process is **how** a group or individual men are handling the communication—who talks, how much, who talks to whom.

In this chapter we are going to be talking about process, the dynamic that goes on between the members in the group.

Patterns of communication are some of the more obvious aspects of the group process to observe. Examples:

1. Who talks? For how long? How often?
2. Who do the men look at when they talk?
   a. Singling out others as possible supporters.
   b. Scanning the group.
   c. No one.
3. Who talks after whom, or who interrupts whom.
4. What style of communication is used (assertions, questions, tone of voice, gestures, etc.)?

Personal behavior process is less obvious than the above communication patterns, and it is largely what we are going to examine on the next two pages.

The following overview of common roles and group behaviors may be valuable to you in becoming a better leader or member of your group. If you are able to recognize these roles and behaviors, this list will give you direction in making useful interventions and promoting increased awareness in your group.

Roles and behavior processes in a group can be viewed in terms of their purpose and function. There are generally three types: task, maintenance, and self.

1. Task-focused behavior involves moving the group's process toward getting something tangible decided or accomplished. The following are task roles:

Initiating. Proposing tasks or goals; defining a problem; suggesting a procedure or ideas for solving a problem. Example: *"Getting to know each other better socially seems to be something I hear guys wanting; perhaps we could organize a picnic together."*

Seeking information or opinion. Requesting facts; eliciting relevant information about a group concern; asking for suggestions or ideas. Example: *"There seems to be doubt here about summer meetings; does anyone have specific ideas about how to work around vacations and general lazy time?"*

Giving information or opinion. Offering facts; providing relevant information about group concerns; stating a brief solution; giving suggestions or ideas. Example: *"I think we could go to an every-other-week basis until September and have one of those meetings be a member-hosted barbecue."*

Clarifying or elaborating. Interpreting or reflecting ideas and suggestions; clearing up confusions; laying out alternatives and issues for the group to accept or reject. Example: *"I'm getting the idea that our group wants to stay connected, yet not feel obligated for the summer, and that social gatherings will serve both purposes."*

Summarizing. Pulling together related ideas; restating suggestions after the group has discussed them; offering decisions or conclusions for the group to accept or reject. Example: *"I'm hearing that guys want more time to discuss and work on issues and that meeting more often is a possibility."*

Consensus testing. Sending up "trial balloons" to see if the group is nearing a conclusion; checking with the group to see how much agreement has been reached. Example: *"Sounds like the group generally wants to extend our weekly ending time to ten-thirty. Is that a consensus?"*

2. Maintenance-focused behavior involves facilitating an individual's process or the group's development. The following are maintenance roles:

Encouragement. Being friendly, warm, and responsive to the other men and to their contributions; showing regard by giving them an opportunity for recognition. Example: *"I liked very much and acknowledge your courage for what you just said about yourself as a father."*

Expressing feelings. Sensing feelings, moods, and relationships within the group; sharing feelings with other members. Example: *"I'm feeling apprehensive and scared about this topic we've been discussing and think this may be true for most of us."*

Harmonizing. Attempting to reconcile disagreement; reducing tension by inviting men to explore their differences. Example: *"There seems to be some powerful conflict between Mike and Chuck. Perhaps if you guys would talk more about your feelings around this issue, we could learn why you two are so passionate about your positions."*

Compromising. Offering to compromise one's position; admitting error; disciplining oneself to maintain group cohesion. Example: *"After hearing your ideas, Steve, about more personal sharing time, I'm willing to let go of my desire for more structured learning exercises."*

Gatekeeping. Attempting to keep communication channels open; facilitating the participation of others; suggesting procedures for sharing the discussion of problems. Example: *"I'm concerned that some guys aren't getting into this discussion of sexuality. Perhaps if we each share about our first kiss or when we discovered masturbation, it will open some doors."*

Setting standards. Expressing standards for the group to achieve; applying the standards in evaluating group process and development. Example: *"We seem to be doing too much heady theorizing lately. I want us to share more personal feelings. Do you agree and how can we do so?"*

3. Self-focused behavior is primarily aimed at meeting personal needs and/or goals without regard for the group. The examples here are **unspoken thoughts**, which if actually shared would be a step toward more strength in that area:

Dependency. Leaning on others to the detriment of the group. Example: *"I can't get along without you guys, I need you, help me."*

Feminism beginning to work its way into every crack and crevice of society.

Counter-dependency. Resisting anyone in the group that represents authority. Example: *"I don't need anyone, especially you, Mister know-it-all, father figure, big shot."*

Fighting. Controlling or asserting personal dominance to reinforce one's ego or sense of safety. Example: *"This group isn't going anywhere; it should have more discussion of men's rights."*

Withdrawing. Psychologically leaving the discomfort of the group. Example: *"I don't think I belong here and I sure hope nobody forces me to say anything. And why do they call this a 'men's group' and not a 'boys' group,' anyway?"*

Subgrouping. Seeking out supporters forming together for emotional protection and support. Example: *"At least I know a couple of guys in this group like me who might stand up against those other guys."*

Note: Subgrouping is also a very common, healthy, and normal part of a group's development. It becomes dysfunctional to the degree that the subgroups become a place to hide out from the larger group.

A dynamic group activity

The above information may be useful in recognizing personal dynamics or motivations that may exist in your group. For a group activity, you might discuss what roles various men are assuming in your group. This can be a positive way to practice giving feedback and doing a group assessment.

"If contemporary men can take the task of their own initiation from Boyhood to Manhood as seriously as did their tribal forebears, then we may witness the *end* of the *beginning* of our species, instead of the *beginning* of the *end*."

—Robert Moore and Douglas Gillette,
King, Warrior, Magician, Lover

PART FIVE
MEN'S READINGS AND INFORMATION

"No magical redemption from outside of human life will let us break through. The work that has to be done is our work, but we are better equipped for it than we have been led to believe. To move ourselves beyond selfishness, we already have what is required. We already *are* what is required. We are human and we have each other."

—Alfie Kohn, *The Brighter Side of Human Nature*

"Friendship may be the best antidote for the alienation that is the inevitable result of corporate and professional styles of life."

—Sam Keen, *Fire in the Belly*

WE'RE NOT READY YET, BUT SOON:
Exploring the Edge of Maleness

Article by **Danaan Parry**

I've read this article dozens of times since its publication in the 1985 summer edition of *In Context*. Its joyous poetic nature expresses the essence of healthy manhood. When the time is right, read it aloud in your group, then discuss it, or better yet, go camping together. Danaan Parry is one of my heroes. Twenty years ago, after beginning a promising career as a nuclear physicist, he decided that building bombs was the wrong way to promote peace, and he became a clinical psychologist. Shortly thereafter, while working with Mother Teresa in Bombay, he realized his mission was to be a conflict-resolution/peace professional. He cofounded Earthstewards Network, which has outreach programs around the world, and began a training program called Warriors of the Heart, through which he now teaches other men the skills necessary to become positive changemakers.
—Bill Kauth

I can see Andy through the fire. He's hopping from one foot to the other in some rhythmic way, to some perhaps ancient beat inside of him. The flames from our driftwood campfire leap thirty feet in the air, and I am starting to feel that feeling again. It's the one that I feel every time I huddle around a campfire, and I get very hot on one side of my body and very cold on the other side. Suddenly I am no longer in this time, this place. I am somewhere, some ancient place and I am naked and my muscles and tendons resonate to some primal energy and I am man at the awakening of . . . I don't know what. I lose it at that point, as though I am not supposed to remember. Not yet!

And so here we are, Andy and me, and Bob, and a half dozen other men. It is spring equinox and we have come together to spend the night on this beach. Another group, all women, have chosen to spend the night on the mountain ridge. Separately, we will evoke the energies of our gender: we will try to open to our own, brothers to brothers, sisters to sisters, beyond role and game and expectation. We will try. We will use ritual and dance and story and whatever we can to explore who is this being, man; who is this being, woman. And we have talked of what to do in the morning. An agreement—we, the men, will come to a meadow between the ocean shore and the mountain ridge. The women, too, will come. We will meet, and see what happens. We will try.

But now it's midnight, or one, or two, and my brothers and I are hot on one side and cold on the other. I am me and not me; I am very new and very old, and through it all I know that I am man. It feels so incredibly good, incredibly right, to be here with these men in this way.

Later, the poet Robert Bly would give me a framework for these feelings, as he reintroduces me to the masculine archetype of the "wildman." This aspect of the male being is a deep, subconscious source of primary energy which, Bly contends, has been ignored by men in our desire to integrate the softer, more intuitive feminine aspects into our personas. Certainly, the macho, hostile behaviors of most present male cultural stereotypes are in sore need of balancing. This can be done, and in many ways is being done, by men who are allowing the feminine aspects (that each of us men has within us) to emerge and enrich our lives. Beneath this outer male/female balance, though, lies a more primary power source that must have means of expression for wholeness to be experienced. Bly calls this the "wildman" in men.

For now though, there is only the heat of the fire and my brothers and it is enough. I am full as I have not been full for a very, very long time.

Now the sun shows its first glow over the ridge, and Andy is pulling me toward the water's edge. And now we are naked and running through the ocean surf and screaming. God, I love to scream. I mean *really* scream. I'm freezing. The March Pacific Ocean laps against my genitals, and the morning sun paints its way over the ridge, across the lagoon and spills over my trembling body. From my belly button up, I am golden and warm, from there down I am sea-green and cold. And that ancient feeling is with me again.

From somewhere in me, from a place so deep I had not known it existed in me, there comes forth another scream. Not from my throat, my voice, my lungs, but from my belly, from some dark, deep cave in the bowels of me. The scream explodes from me, an orgasm of emotion. You may have heard it! It was that loud, that powerful. My brothers stood frozen, drinking me in. Then, their screams echoed mine as we bathed the beach in joy. We *frolicked*. Have you ever seen grown men *frolic?* I thought my heart would burst.

And then the awareness of what had happened sank into me. There, in this freezing water, for the first moment in my life, I felt *man* and felt no shame for it. Yes, for all my life, at some level just below my conscious awareness, I had felt shame about being a man. Why? Perhaps because of some images of men as the "violent ones," the destroyers, the war-makers. I don't know; all I know is that it had been there, this low-grade chronic inability to fully embrace who I am. And now it was gone. Purged. Released.

The molten, churning powerhouse of primal energy that lies within my maleness is neither good nor evil—it is simply pure energy. My consciousness is the force that decides how this vast store of primal energy is used. And because I and so many of my brothers are growing in consciousness, we are becoming ready to own our "wildman." We are beginning to honor the powerful inner broadsword of creative action that is our way of manifesting Light in physical form.

For the first time all night, we brothers shared words, as we excitedly talked of our fear and shame and confusion. Of the relationships that were "supposed" to bring us happiness, the success that was promised to bring us fulfillment. And now we, here, committing ourselves, our man-selves, to use our strength, our will, our power to create not destroy, to love not fear, to contribute what only man-energy can contribute to the creation of a peace-filled future for our world.

We are do-ers, and we are learning to direct our do-ing energy in ways of service and wholeness. Gandhi, Martin Luther King, and Anwar Sadat are glowing examples of men who have owned their inner broadsword.

It was time to go to the meadow. The women would be there. Perhaps some clarity about the next step would be there. In our circle before we left the beach, we shared how hard it was to leave, to let go of this togetherness-beyond-ego. And we shared how important it is to keep our commitments. And so we walked together toward the meadow.

We could see the women coming down the trail from the mountain. Images of warm hugs and soft smells were with me now. But as we approached the women, I noticed that my body was beginning to close, just a bit. My shoulders were hunching forward, just a bit. My freely swinging hips were becoming just a bit more controlled, more proper. Others noticed their body responses too. We were returning.

Then we were together, men and women, people who care deeply for each other. We were looking at each other, saying nothing. For a long time. One of the women broke the difficult silence. She said, "Not yet."

We all knew what she meant. We turned and walked away. No more words were spoken for many hours. Feelings of sadness and rightness swept through me. We had touched something during that night, something so deep and vital that for me, man, and her, woman, to attempt to come together *at that level* would have been impossible. For now.

There will come a time when men and women *will* come together at that level. But first men, as men, and women, as women, must explore the depths, the incredible depths of who they are. They/we must risk and open and explore and claim the woman-power and the man-power that live in that cave deep within and yet beyond ourselves. We have only just begun.

When men and women have done that work and then come together, the co-creation from that union will move us from where we are to where we were meant to be.

I ask myself, "What is this *man*-power, this deeper manifestation of who-I-am-as-man?" And the words that come to me are *create, risk, explore, challenge, thrust, go beyond.* And more—all having that old, old feeling in me that I have come to associate, in my societal experience, with "getting in trouble." Hmmmm.

The trouble with men . . . I'm walking along a beach, just relaxing and enjoying the day. No one around except the sea gulls and maybe a harbor seal. My car is up on the road, and so I begin the ascent to the top of the cliff, up the gradual, nicely laid-out State Park trail. But then my eye catches a glimpse of some interesting rocks to my left. I'll bet I could make it up that way. It's steep, no trail, loose rocks. What if I fell? Why take the chance? But in me there is no question. My pants get filthy, my hand gets cut, it's an hour longer and I love it. What's that all about?

I'm driving a motorcycle along the coast highway. The bike is humming, every one of the hundreds of little parts performing just right, to create a harmony, and I as driver am a part of that harmony. At the same moment I am in charge of this assemblage and only a part of it, a piece of the whole. Is this just macho bullshit, or do I really experience a living connection to all of this? I feel a balance of me and us; me and the machine and the *us* that emerges from all of the parts working just right.

There's a curve coming up. I can see the road far ahead of it. If I take the curve at this speed there's a risk. Five miles an hour faster and I know I'll lose it. Five miles an hour slower asks nothing of me, of us. So what, there's nobody around to prove anything to. But I know already, beyond questions, beyond analysis, what I will do. I begin to feel that old body response to my adrenal glands doing their job. I can feel my parasympathetic nervous system flipping to *alert*, to "on-line, everybody . . . all hands on deck." My biocomputer shifts to high-speed data analysis: "probability of patch of gravel around curve . . . probability of error in judgment about clear road ahead . . . awareness of amount of tread on tire . . ." My vision clears, focuses, soft eyes to take in the big picture, muscles alert and relaxed at the same time. We're going in. Not me, we. Every cell in me, every gene, every bolt and piston and spoke.

And the curve is behind us now. *We* goes back to *me*, and me develops a cold sweat, and I can feel my left brain start to ask questions and make judgments: "You ass, you hot dog, you macho jerk. Why do you do those dumb things?"

Maybe because it's one of the very few ways that my culture allows me, that I allow me, to give life to an ancient need.

You see, it is the nature of masculinity to feel and to desire the experience of intensity, of living at the edge, of challenge and risk-taking. That is not all we are, but it is a natural, deep, wonderful part of who we are. This is the "inner fire" that infuses our actions with aliveness.

I have talked to so many Vietnam vets, my brothers who have experienced kill and/or be killed. They, most of them, ache. They are lost. And they whisper to me of a terrible awareness that on the battlefield, facing probable death, they felt, for the first time in their life, fully alive. And every experience since then has had a meaningless, mediocre taste to it. How are we to make sense of all this? And we *must!*

We cannot simplistically demand that men stop this foolishness and think it will work. It's so much deeper than that. Do you think that there have not been "peace movements" for thousands of years? Do you think that women have not been begging and demanding men for thousands of years to evolve beyond their dominating, oppressive, violent behavior? Do you think that simply beating our swords into plowshares will change anything? What will we do with all those plowshares?

There is an intensity to maleness. It has something to do with pushing limits, with trying the untryable, with risking what is for what could be. And it has caused a lot of trouble. This intensity has manifested in ways that pit us against one another, that inflate or deflate our personal egos, and that objectify whatever or whomever gets in our way. So what to do?

In recent years we have tried, to one degree or another, to let go of these macho, manipulative ways of expressing our maleness. We, some of us, have tried to embrace that softer, gentler, intuitive "feminine" nature that surely lives within each man. It is a worthwhile and necessary movement.

And now, after some difficult-wonderful years of exploring my yin, my receptive nature, I am beginning to hear the soft wisdom of my inner voice, my intuitive self. It whispers to me that my next journey in awareness is not toward androgyny, rather to deeper levels of maleness. To explore that creative, passionate risker, that limit-pusher that burns to live 100 percent, beyond macho, beyond any need to prove his worth.

We must never "cork the volcano" of our male intensity. (Corked volcanoes explode.) We must develop the clarity and the self-love to direct its awesome power for good. Our world cries out for men to move beyond their role-playing and beyond their shame, and to unlock that deep fertile maleness that lives in us. Humankind hungers for this good, grounded male energy, just as surely as it hungers for clear, deep, powerful woman energy. And the integration of those creative forces will birth something very new, very wonderful.

Not yet, but soon!

To find out about Danaan Parry's books, write to:

Sunstone Publications
RD4, Box 700A
Cooperstown, NY 13326
or call (800) 327-0306

To learn more about the Earthstewards Network, write to:

P.O. Box 10697
Bainbridge Island, WA 98110

Reprinted from *In Context, A Quarterly of Humane Sustainable Culture*
Subscriptions $18 per year; single issues $5
P.O. Box 11470, Bainbridge Island, WA 98110

THEY ALL DIED IN THE WAR

Article by **Bill Kauth**

This article is a theory rooted in my personal experience.

The mystery: As a man devoted to doing men's work, I'm constantly invited to explore the question "where did our fathers go?" I know well that current wisdom says our dads lost their sense of manhood in meaningless work that resulted from the industrial revolution. But I sensed there was more. Within one generation something dramatic happened. They were gone! Where did they go? The more I learn about the archetypal warrior, the more I think our fathers all died in World War II.

Personal history of the mystery: On the Fourth of July, 1988, I was alone watching a TV movie on the building of the Vietnam war memorial. The show, called *To Heal A Nation*, was a recreation of Vietnam veteran Jan Scruggs' personal and political struggle to get the memorial built. A way into the story I began feeling, in my breathing, an impending sadness, which soon became tears and sobbing. I was confused by my unexpected deep emotional response.

The next day I told my friend, Doug, about my emotional experience, and he told me that both he and his wife had also cried as they watched the same program. He speculated that it was a natural grief reaction, as he had known men who had been killed in Vietnam. It almost made sense, except that I had only one distant acquaintance in college who had died in Vietnam. My response had been way too strong.

It plugged me into remembering a similar response three years before, while reading *National Geographic*'s account of the building of the Vietnam memorial wall. It was a very technical account of the political and aesthetic conflicts surrounding the building of the memorial, yet I cried through damn near the whole dry article.

As a psychotherapist, I've trained myself in emotional awareness. These emotional responses perplexed me. My reactions were not logical. Yet they were very viscerally real. My body knew something I didn't. It was a mystery and I wanted an answer.

Nearly everyone I talked to within my age range (thirty-five to fifty) who had read the same article or had been to the wall felt the same emotional response whether they were veterans, draft dodgers, men, or women. There was some **emotional commonality** here. And while many people had some specific rationale for their responses, none fit generally. I tucked it away as one of those mysteries that would come to light someday.

The theory: A year later this mystery, which I had carried for over three years, popped open. I knew from reading, and from seventeen years of men's work, that manhood as it once had been known had been fading since the industrial age replaced the agrarian age. As our great-great-grandfathers moved from the farms to the cities into essentially meaningless work, they lost that strong male identity a man finds in his work. A man often identifies with what he does or builds out in the world, external to himself. It was this focus he passed on to his sons. Men's ability to pass on a meaningful sense of manhood has been waning for over 200 years.

Then something big and fast happened with World War II. It seemed to strip away what was left of our fathers' ability to pass on to us whatever sense of manhood remained. I knew this from years of observing and talking to many men as well as from reading accounts of men's pain, anger, and confusion around their sense of manhood.

One sunny morning while discussing shame with my friend, Tony, the pieces of the puzzle jumped into place. I imagined the correlation between my own inexplicable grief feelings about Vietnam, the mystery of our lost WWII dads, the women's movement, and the insane fact that we humans have at least enough bombs to destroy all life on the planet twenty times over and that we keep building more of them every damn day.

The answer seems to be **shame from dishonoring the archetype.** I think it is important at this point to define "shame" and consider male "archetypes" with a focus on the warrior.

Shame: I've seen shame defined as the painful belief in one's basic defectiveness as a human being. I learned about shame and how it is different from guilt from a 1986 article by Francis Baumli in *Transitions* (a men's rights newsletter). He said, "Shame is often referred to as a void. A person who is ashamed feels empty inside, without ballast, lacking a sense of self-centeredness or emotional certainty. Shame is something quite indeterminate and unspecifiable. Shame is felt in terms of what one is as opposed to what one does, which is guilt."

Shame is difficult to grapple with because it has no specific form. Attempts at dealing with it tend to leave one feeling helpless. So shame is much more likely than guilt to persist as a toxic, crippling feeling compensated for by an anger which, if turned inward, becomes self-destructive. And shame is **always secret.** Nobody talks about it.

The "warrior" archetype: I believe the male archetypes exist as part of the male psyche. According to C. G. Jung, archetypes are "the hidden foundations of the conscious mind . . . the two-million-year-old man that is in all of us . . . an inherited mode of functioning." The archetype has existed 100 or 1000 times before, so the imprint is left in our minds.

Thanks to Robert Moore and Robert Bly, we've come to know some of these archetypal "patterns of behavior" as the king, warrior, magus, lover, blacksmith, and clown. Another one is the natural man, whom some of us have come to value deeply as the "wildman." It is when we are in touch with this one that we know instinctively we are men.

The archetypal warrior is the keeper of order and safety. He serves the sacred king. He is loyal, faithful, and disciplined. He is dedicated to his cause and unswerving in his mission, be he an author, musician, businessman, or doctor.

When we open ourselves to look deeply into our inner warrior who has existed for thousands of years, it feels right. Every man is intuitively in touch with that raw masculine energy that protected and preserved our distant ancestors. His warriorship was meaningful work. It was the essence of who he was, and it felt right. However, there is a shadow side.

World War II: Our dads took on the awesome mission of WWII with great courage, and they were wounded, deep inside. They were in the first fully automated war. The sense of genuine "warriorship" was grotesquely distorted or absent. These were men (like their fathers, doing meaningless work) who were operating cold machines that delivered death miles away or miles below. And the final blow, the climactic culmination of WWII, was the atomic vaporization of thousands of men, women, and children.

Our fathers fought WWII against the covertly rageful, grandiose, narcissistic insanity of Hitler's Germany. This enemy was made up of men so severely damaged emotionally as to be possessed by the shadow warrior. Cynical and without compassion, they released the Mars energy of war in ways that violated every code of honor a warrior has. I suspect that, in the way members of a dysfunctional family get drawn into its craziness and secrets, our fathers too got close to that shadow warrior.

Here is the subtle part: Beneath the rationale, beneath the good, solid, logical reasons (Pearl Harbor, stopping Hitler), is the reality that they killed millions of people. Beyond the rationales that "the enemy did it too, we had to protect ourselves, we saved one million American lives," lies the fact that they did it. Beyond whatever reasons they used to justify it, they did it. And they stuffed it down inside themselves. Well below conscious awareness lay their horrible secret, and there they kept it.

True warriorship is a way of being that includes integrity and honor. It is a highly intimate experience. I've read of samurai warriors who could face off in mortal combat for many hours and be so utterly present and in contact with one another that neither would swing their swords. The warriors of millennia **faced** their opponent, respected him. War became a ritual process of respectful men. The warrior knew who he was, why he was doing what he was doing, and he felt good about himself.

Our fathers did not feel good about themselves as warriors because they were mechanics operating machines of death. They were part of the slaughter of millions (all rationale aside) and so were the folks back home who made the bullets and saved the tin foil. Their spirits died in the unconscious shame associated with dishonoring the archetypal warrior. The shame of WWII was secret. They rarely, if ever, talked about their experience of the war. Later they threw themselves into work, bottled spirits, or other addictions to salve the shame.

Warriorship and manhood died an inglorious death. Civilization had evolved into an inhuman killing machine, and manhood died in the gears.

The women's movement: With the demise of manhood there was a void of male energy in the Western world. Authentic male energy was in very short supply. Because nature abhors a vacuum, the deficit of male spiritual and emotional energy led to several social responses.

Wives went crazy with frustration, living with men who came home to them spiritually dead. They felt powerless to do anything about it. In their desperation, too often, they tried making their sons into the man they were missing.

Sons took to the skies, emulating Peter Pan, the puer aeternus or eternal boy living out various playboy and spiritual life-styles to compensate for what their environment lacked. Growing up without an emotionally alive father and experiencing the emotional incest with Mom made intimate relationships with both men and women difficult.

Daughters' attempt to fill the void by becoming as like men as possible was the most dramatic manifestation. The women's movement was, beyond all the rationale (unequal pay, men had all the power, housework is slavery), a deeply felt need to balance out what was missing. In some ways young women tried to be men. So desperate was their need for male energy that they attempted to create it themselves. Most found it very unrewarding and have created ways to embrace their feminine selves again.

Overall, I think the most socially destructive result of the male energy void was Mom's anger toward Dad, which our generation unconsciously took in. It became the social prejudice against men. Man bashing is still acceptable. Women often admit that among themselves they rarely have much good to say about men. The saddest part is that too many men hold the same prejudice. They do not like men.

> "The warrior's nuclear shield doesn't protect us anymore. We are all huddled together on a worldwide battlefield, brothers and sisters in a nuclear family, one race, indivisible, with destruction and fallout for all."
> —Sam Keen,
> *Fire in the Belly*

The bomb: The bomb? What bomb? After WWII the number of bombs kept growing, despite public knowledge that we were long past the amount it would take to eliminate human life on the planet. Shame is always a secret, so the absurdity and nihilism of the bomb had to be kept secret or justified in some way.

As world alliances rearranged themselves into two superpower camps, each side could logically point to the other as the enemy from which they needed to be protected. That protected the secret. It was the same secret for both sides, rooted in the same shame.

The "Atoms for Peace" program built nuclear power plants, and men felt they could logically say, "See, this atomic stuff isn't so bad; it produces electric power." They, too, protected the secret. Our legacy is cost-ineffective, billion-dollar water boilers with toxic waste products that we can't get rid of.

The healing: As long as our fathers stayed in power, the secret remained. Their shadow of shame was so great that they were willing to face death rather than look at it. Now something has changed. Perhaps the shame of their sons in Vietnam opened the door. Since the war ended, 50,000 Vietnam veterans have committed suicide. Perhaps this agonizing fact engendered a deep, quiet feeling of empathy. Perhaps they could see for the first time their own pain in the mirror of their sons: men coming home broken from a similar war. This time there was no rationale, no reason to be there. The shame could not be denied with good reasons.

On a spring day in 1989, Robert Bly said, "Warriors do not make war. It is the lack of connectedness to the warrior archetype that causes war."

Men are taking back their archetypal warrior spirit. I believe that the ending of the "cold war" in Europe was the shadow coming into the light. Some men are looking inside and consciously living out the warrior archetype. Devoted to a mission greater than themselves, they engage in conflict, and they trust their use of power. They are no longer afraid of their inner warrior.

Tears of joy come to my eyes as I think, for the first time in my life, that we may survive. Yet I know too well that those bombs are still out there, and that Mother Earth is badly wounded. She will need several million men with true warrior spirit rooted in a mission of service to heal her. So, warrior brothers, let us complete our battles within and together take joy in the battles without!

Addendum

After this article ran in winter 1990, I got several calls and letters from people thanking me for the insights they gained from it. My journalist friends tell me the response was far higher than normal, suggesting it somehow touched a nerve.

In 1991, I spent some time in Europe and continued my research, asking men from Germany, Austria, and France questions about their missing fathers and shame. They knew immediately what I was talking about.

I also got to know several people who were affiliated with an ashram in Poona, India, where between three and four thousand people visit at all times doing spiritual work. I was fascinated to learn that the Germans are the single largest ethnic group of spiritual seekers in Poona. And I was stunned to find out that, given my theory about World War II, the Japanese are the second largest ethnic group.

And, as the fates would have it, on the train to Paris I met a Japanese man. As we were sitting in the dining car getting to know each other, he told me he worked in Tokyo for IBM and I told him I did men's work. And with virtually no explanation I expressed my interest in how life was for Japanese men. Without missing a beat he shared that since World War II, it has been very hard for men, because they had lost their sense of spirit.

This article was published in the Winter 1990 issue of the quarterly:
Wingspan: Journal of the Male Spirit
P.O. Box 23550
Brightmoor Station
Detroit, MI 48223
(313) 273-4330

Write to get on their mailing list.
Free, donations gratefully accepted.

THE WOUNDS OF AQUARIUS:

The Loss of Fierceness and the Fear of Power

Article by **Gabriel Heilig**

Of all the articles on men's work I have read over the last decade, this one, printed in *Pathways* (Washington, D.C.) in spring 1990, best gets to the heart of where men have been and where we need to go. It's a passionate overview of the need for nice guys to go into their "shadows," reclaim their fierceness and power, and as initiated men . . . go into the world to put out the fire. I suggest that in highly motivated men's support groups this process is accelerated. Sink your teeth into this article!
—Bill Kauth

So many die before they awaken.

—Sufi saying

As we breathe and walk, the world is burning around us in a blaze of cruel contradictions. If ever there was an age of contrasts, surely ours is the age. For here are: more light, more darkness; more privilege, more poverty; more hope, more hazard; more wisdom, and more foolishness. On one hand, we are the Age of Aquarius, the vaunted "New Age." (Or so we like to imagine ourselves in our pre-millennial grandeur.) Yet we also live in what may be the most dysfunctional society the world has ever seen—so much so, that either we will clean it up in the next ten to twenty years or not have to worry about leaving any posterity.

It's been about a century since human beings in our part of the planet lived in a culture that was whole, and most of them were killed or shoveled onto reservations. By "whole," I mean a culture in which the shadow elements of human nature are visible, not split off or projected onto others, but accepted as part of the human landscape. Like many dysfunctional families, we of the New Age Generation also suffer from this splitting-off and denial process. Our darker feelings are stuffed into the bulging shadows we drag unseen behind us. Like children who've been watching too many Spielberg movies, we enjoy imagining we will enter world history as the Heroes of the Coming Light. But where are our Knights of the Shadows? Who guards our darkness? Or is it all light back there?

When treating a dysfunctional family, psychologists note that grandiose fantasies can be seen as compensating reactions masking a deep sense of inner shame. And as with a family, so perhaps with a culture. And so perhaps with ours. For we have plundered the Native Americans, plundered the land itself, and enslaved others to plunder it for us; yet still we parade before the mirrors of our vanity with purchases from our malls.

Such vanity is the tinderbox of history's bonfires.

I offer the thought that we might use fewer Heroes of the Light and a few more Heroes of the Darkness, men and women willing to explore their personal lost continents, those shadow places buried so deeply beneath us that we no longer know what ground we are standing on, like a landfill so huge it looks like the Earth itself. How can we stand on such ground and expect to climb securely toward the angels? The image mocks itself.

In the New Age, we prize ecstasy, love, beauty, and purity. Yet around us we see misery, meanness, ugliness, and filth. The paradox is severe. So many malls—and so little meaning. For we cannot escape the condition of life as it is, or ourselves as we are. And if we do not accept responsibility for the world we have made and the selves we have made it with, we risk adding our naiveté and numbness to the common blindness which refuses to see what's in front of its nose. If we paste forgiveness and love on top of our fear and shame, what have we accomplished? Have we healed our wounds—or just buried them more deeply? I cannot speak for women, but I think now that for Aquarian men a certain fierceness and rigorous self-inquiry are in order.

After twenty-five years of Aquarian explorations, I wear the title of "New Age man" with mixed feelings. For as I have watched the paisley visions of the '60s and '70s become the ecstasy industries of the 1980s, I've felt something missing in the New Age attitude, especially for men. I know that I missed it, and many men whom I know speak of having missed it also. What's missing feels like a visceral intensity, one that manifests as a loss of fierceness, and its flip side, the fear of power.

Fierceness—hardly an Aquarian virtue. Our New Age accepts mildness more readily than intensity. To many Aquarian ears, fierceness probably sounds more like savagery than what it is: an innate element of human nature. If you doubt it, try taking a spoon away from an infant who's got one in her grip, and you'll know what fierceness is. It's not about muscle size. And it's not about scaring anybody. It's about being fully present with our power to claim. Or as a friend once put it, "It's one of the cornerstones supporting the rapture in being alive." For aliveness **is** fierce. That's part of what **keeps** it alive.

Fierceness is one of the primary colors we need to paint ourselves onto the canvas of life. It may even be more than a color. It may be the brush itself. For to live as a conscious adult is a willed risk, the risk of giving up illusions.

The illusion that we can pay our rent with our dreams.

The illusion that adulthood follows automatically after childhood.

The illusion that good intentions lead to good results.

The illusion that following the rules will keep us safe.

The illusion that there is one True Path, and that someone else not only will guide us onto it but will choose it for us.

No—we must choose. In Sartre's phrase, we are "condemned to freedom," exploring our lives as if on a map with no marked roads or borders. We must follow our own sense of what is true, defining whatever claims we make or boundaries we will honor, not because what lies on our side of a boundary is any "better" that what's on the other side. Only children think like that. Grown men and women know something else: that nothing is better on **either** side, but we know which side **we** are on.

I think Aquarian men particularly have not summoned our power sufficiently to define the boundaries we will claim and honor. For men, the challenge of heroism as described in mythology is not to attack across a boundary, but to defend our side of it. What is crucial is the **willingness**, even more than the ability to defend it. For in that willingness is born the fierceness which carries a man into battle over the walls of his fears. What matters in that moment is not whether he wins or loses or even whether he lives or dies, but that he fights or creates with everything that is in him and that he is fierce with the flavor of his own strength, whatever that may be. A man may be a bear or a falcon, a dolphin or a fox, an ass or a lion, but he must not be afraid to reach down into his primal sources to find the wildness he needs.

It's been said that among the traditionally honored tasks of men are: to embark on ventures wise and foolish, to play tricks, to make trouble, to awaken the emotional bodies of younger men, and to individuate, not only from others but from our childhoods.

Alas. American culture does all it can to keep us childlike. Our popular imagery isn't about men or women, but of Yup-Boys and Yup-Girls "going for the gusto" in a media cartoon with all of life's failure, difficulty, and boredom airbrushed out. New Age, Old Age, we are the Packaged Society, even in our identities. No wonder the work of adulthood gets no respect. It's low on the Gusto Meter.

But hey, somebody'd better do it.

The world's on fire.

For those of us who came up the easy way, in the American Mall culture that spawned the New Age Emporium, the gate to fierceness often is masked with smiles, soft tones, and "niceness." In the New Age, we're always supportive and pleasant, right? I mean—let's not argue. Let's have a bowl of brown rice, close our eyes, find our centers, and come to consensus. Can't we rise above all this negative energy about fierceness?

The answer is: we can—at a price. Unfortunately, for men this price is high. For the more a man surrenders or refuses to activate his own fierceness, the more he invites the danger of being blown around in life and by our own culture, which is savage and which demands fierceness and cunning to survive in it—much less to improve or transform it. For a man to deny his own wildness can become self-destructive, at many levels. And if a woman denies this necessity in a man, she may find herself complaining to friends that she always winds up with wimps. But many of these "wimps" are would-be tigers who never learned to roar. A low tolerance for fierceness blurs the emotional contrasts and softens the vivid edges in the contact between a woman and a man. Chords make harmony, but chords require an ability to hear different notes, and to let them be played.

The loss of fierceness. The fear of power. They form a curious wound: softening us where we should be strong, and numbing us where we should be most alive. I can illustrate with a few personal reflections.

Once upon a time in graduate school, a group of us sat in a circle during class, passing around a turquoise beach ball while chanting a rhyme. (The year was 1969, so you can believe that this actually happened in grad school.) Whenever one round of our chant ended, the person with the beach ball would have all the group's power. For a full minute he or she could order the group to do whatever he/she wished. Well, one minute of naked power can be an eternity. Almost without exception, whoever got the Power Ball would try to give it away as soon as possible.

I saw something flash across my inner mirror during that deceptively simple game, something about how I avoid opening to my own power and using it unashamedly. To get past my fear about it, I've had to learn I can plunge my hand into my own power-source to let it up and out. But until I do, my fear feels like ice. Yet once I plunge in, the fear becomes watery and easy to pierce.

But back then in the late '60s, I was moving in another direction. Like many other men, I was tuning in to my feminine feelings. Women seemed to like this approach and we enjoyed "flowing" together. I didn't have to win anyone's love by bringing home the bacon. Tofu would do, from the co-op. New Age manhood seemed pretty easy and undemanding. And that, it now turns out, was the problem.

Looking back, it seems to me this attitude kept me in what I would call the Women's House, following women's emotional lead. Since I wasn't much in touch with my own feelings, I let theirs define mine. I stuffed my rage and burned in secret, exploding when someone got near a land mine I didn't even know was there. Nor did I manage my relationships with women very actively. Instead, it seemed all I had to do, or really knew how to do, was not be too frightening. And since as a "nice Jewish boy" I'd never been aware of frightening anybody, this arrangement was fine with me.

In 1968, Vietnam swept me into its vortex. Teaching near Chicago, I was shielded from the draft by a college teaching deferment—that is, until I wrote my draft board a brash letter announcing that even if I didn't have a deferment I still wouldn't fight in Vietnam. The draft board wrote back: "1-A," and the chase was on. There were visits to ACLU lawyers, a hearing with my draft board to argue my case, and when that failed, I flunked the mental test during the draft physical. Yet I noticed that even while I kept eluding my draft board and shuddering at the thought of fighting in Vietnam, another part of me longed to go through boot camp, to test myself among other men, to feel the bonding of a shared struggle. It was the fierceness I wanted, not the fighting. The warriorship, not the war.

Some years later, I collaborated with a good friend (a former Army captain and Vietnam veteran, oddly enough) in writing a book about what then was being called "men's liberation." Our book was titled *Tenderness Is Strength: From Machismo to Manhood.* Today I would change that title, as I think tenderness is **not** strength. Strength sometimes may have the quality of tenderness, and even fierceness may have some tenderness in it, for often it arises from a desire to protect what we love. Yet we aren't fierce in order to be tender. We are fierce because something we love is at stake.

In the New Age, however, what is at stake often feels misty and indistinct. Boundaries seem blurred, as though life itself were in soft focus. But life is about stones and fangs, not just nectar and light. There are times when tenderness may not be sharp enough to guard what we love, times when only the courage to face our wounds or our foolishness gives us the chance to go beyond them. It isn't easy to live without the comfort of certainties, formulas, or affirmations—and the New Age is full of prepackaged wisdom tablets ready for sale and delivery. But truth and wisdom are old-fashioned virtues, attained the old-fashioned way. They have to be earned—like manhood itself.

Our society has few initiatory structures by which our psyches can be developed and fulfilled. This challenge is not made any easier in a city like Washington, D.C., where I've lived since 1981, where traditional virtues are buried beneath layers of positioning and power lunching. Odysseus may have voyaged the wine-dark seas home to Ithaca, but in Washington I'm navigating the smog-dark Beltway. To get initiated, men must do it without expecting much help from the majority culture—or from the New Age, for that matter, which can turn initiation into yet another workshop, sedating the struggle with soft music. But there is little that is soft about the desire for individuation or initiation. It is a fierce wish, and like many growth experiences it may require breaking old bonds and reopening old wounds.

The work of creating one's own manhood or womanhood is not easy; probably it never has been. It is mostly secret work, done perhaps with a few friends or accomplices. Yet once we cross the bridge to our inner darkness, we are essentially alone there. We may hear the echoes of men or women chipping or blasting away in their own mineshafts, but the mission is pretty much the same for each of us: to rescue our lost children, down there in the old mines beneath the malls.

Today our predicament is this: the gates of the Old Age are rusting behind us, yet the visionary wings of the New Age are still wet. In a sense, the mineshaft is the safest place to be. It is where our wounds live and where our power can be reclaimed. Some of this may require approaching feelings of fear and disgust at our own cowardice, or shame and rage at having let ourselves down in the past. None of this is easy, but is it any easier to keep living without our power and pretending that we don't notice or don't care? Whatever we choose, one thing is unmistakable: those cries from the mine are coming from our own lost children. They are ours to win or lose.

One problem in going down to them is that we in the New Age tend to look for light, not darkness. It's as though we wanted to play only a piano's high notes, never any low notes; as though nature grew only flowers, never roots struggling for water underground; as though a candlelit meditation room had no sooty basement beneath it. Yet without roots, the flower has no structure or sustenance. Without low notes, the upper octaves are cloying. And without a foundation, the meditation room will cave in.

I know. I've played the high notes and tried not to hear the rest. I've floated in breezes, because I was held by no roots. I've sat in meditation halls, oblivious of the shadows in my own basement. It didn't work. Life came pouring in through all the cracks.

There is in the New Age what I call "premature spirituality": a desire for a kind of purity that denies the natural brutality of the world. And there seems to be a bias in Aquarian thinking that "spiritual" attitudes are better than worldly ones.

I question that. In the classical Indian culture that many Aquarians imagine they emulate, the search for God was begun only **after** one's mundane obligations of family and fortune had been satisfied. After raising a family, husbands and wives would don white clothing, say good-bye to each other, and leave home with begging bowls to accept life's blows on the path toward God. They didn't head for ashrams at age twenty-two. They were seasoned by life before they began their spiritual searching.

But today, it seems, no one can wait. We want God right now, and on our terms. But God's terms are the only ones we get, and we have to find them in the world. We may want to merge back into the white light, to rest in the source. But perhaps soft Aquarian wombs give birth to soft Aquarian wounds.

My question is: why not remain born while we are still alive—alive with the passion of our births?

I came across a proverb once: "Desire is conquered through passion." I think it means that by summoning our fierceness in a given moment, we can release ourselves from the fantasies of our mental desires about the future or our regrets over the past. After all, why desire what **isn't** present if we can have what **is**?

My conviction is that spiritual strength is earned by traveling the path of the world, not by avoiding it—that we are purified by fiercely engaging the world and its passions, not by avoiding them as unholy or impure. Power, money, sex: they do corrupt—and so does the fear of them. The New Age may affirm the angelic above the animal, the mystical above the mundane, but I see little point in ascending before I have learned to stand my ground. Some of what I stand on may be painful, even ugly or demonic. But before I can claim my wholeness, I have a responsibility to introduce my angels to my demons. To keep them split apart disempowers me, just as to ignore what is dark dishonors my pain and what it gave me, and cheapens my compassion for the wounds of others. I believe that to overskip this stage, to blithely transmute unexperienced grief into "bliss," or shame into affirmations, is to pull the wool down over our own eyes and not see that we are turning ourselves into sheep.

I see a difference, a radical and absolute difference, between a "good boy" and a "good man." "Good boys" (and I was one) numb our demons, stuff our rage, and sweetly quote the saints. Because our wounds are tinged with shame and isolation, we dread experiencing what our lives have cost us, either by our own mistakes or by the betrayals of others. Yet as James Hillman has noted in his startling essay, "Betrayal," in *Loose Ends,* until we have been betrayed by life and **have forgiven life for its betrayal of us**, we remain children. For we continue to expect, in John le Carré's words, "that our pleasures and pains will be paid for by our parents."

Our wounds give our humanity its flavor and its bite. Until we dare their murky world, they may seem to us like quicksand. Even to peer into them threatens to suck us down. Yet we may not need to heal our wounds as much as to feel the pain in them, and the joy that has been imprisoned in that pain. To refuse this descent is to refuse our lost kingdoms, our lost crowns, the power that could be ours to stand between our angels and demons and grip them both.

The tone of fierceness is perhaps best described by the French novelist George Sand's comment: "There is a kind of anger which is also one of the most passionate forms of love." To refuse the descent toward our own wounds and the intensity of the fierceness we will find there runs the risk of keeping us naive, numb, and disappointed: another Aquarian soul looking for the workshop that will make him whole again. But there is no such workshop.

There is only the work.

This descent toward our own lost power requires us to commit what we have in order to claim what we **could** have.

Is it worth the journey? Each one of us gets a lifetime to live in that question—and, like it or not, we get to live our answers out.

And in the meantime, the world is burning.

INFORMATION ON

THE NEW WARRIOR TRAINING ADVENTURE

MEN'S WEEKEND

As one of the founders of the New Warrior Training Adventure, I've organized and staffed well over forty of these events, giving myself the opportunity from the beginning to witness the miracles of men providing initiation for each other. Many of the books and tapes in the next chapter, representing what I consider the best in current men's literature, address the need men have today for initiation into manhood by other men.

Chris Harding, editor of *Wingspan: Journal of the Male Spirit,* stated in a recent article that around the turn of the century, fifty percent of American men belonged to at least one men's organization. That has declined greatly until the emergence of the mythopoetic men's movement. He further suggested that the New Warrior Network seems to be one of the emerging fraternal organizations. We are filling the needs of men as did the men's societies of our great-great-grandfathers nearly a century ago.

The work we have been doing through the New Warrior training and follow-up support groups has been of such significant benefit to men that I want to tell you more about our work, in order to plant a seed. If it lands on fertile earth you may choose to experience the training and join the local New Warrior community, or if one does not currently exist, create one.

What are we up to?

In earlier preindustrial cultures, men had role models to learn from and admire. The traditions of manhood were passed down from generation to generation. As civilization supposedly advanced, our fathers, grandfathers, and uncles stopped teaching us how to be men. Role modeling and mentoring became things of the past. Boys were cut off from a deeper sense of who they were as men and became dependent on women to bless their manhood. The very nature of masculinity came under intense scrutiny. Male identity was often mocked or scorned. The New Warrior training was created to fill a need.

How did the New Warrior training begin?

In 1984 three of us from Wisconsin designed the first New Warrior training. We were men who noticed there was no meaningful, shared passage into manhood for men today, nor had there been one for several generations. Feeling that gap in ourselves, we decided to do something about it. We were aiming for a training experience for men that would challenge and educate. Now with eight years of experience, well over 3000 graduates, and the co-creative energies of our brothers from Chicago, Minneapolis, and elsewhere, we've got it. The New Warrior training is an accelerated learning experience that helps men gain purpose, define their mission in life, and face the obstacles that keep them from the fulfillment of that mission.

What it is not . . .

The New Warrior training is not a cult. No dogma. No doctrine. It is not a "survival school" experience. No war games. It is not anti-female. It is not a weekend of psychotherapy.

So what is it?

It is a true initiatory experience. Each man is asked to examine his life as a man. It is an intense self-exploration and healing. On all weekends twenty or more men on staff volunteer their time and skills to guide the new men through the challenging opportunities, including discussions, insights, team games, and ceremonies. There are never more than twenty-five initiates per training.

> "Unless we find the courage, the true warrior's courage, to face ourselves as we are rather than as we hope to be, we will never be able to extricate ourselves from the ancient, persistent riptide of war and violence."
> —Rick Fields,
> *The Code of the Warrior*

Why call it The New Warrior Training?

Other names are possible (The New Man Training, The New Male Weekend), but those names somehow dilute the force of what lies in the deepest recesses of the male psyche. Every man is intuitively in touch with the concept of the warrior: the raw masculine energy that once protected and preserved our distant ancestors. The word "warrior" best describes a powerful spirit in the masculine psyche.

The old dominating, acquisitive warrior is obsolete. The New Warrior is a man living a mission beyond himself. He knows who he is, what he wants, and where he is going. Simply put, he is a man, without guilt, shame, or apology. He has integrity. He holds himself accountable for his own actions. He is wild and gentle, tough and loving, fierce and perceptive. He comes from a tribe of men. He is not a savage. He is a Warrior of the Heart.

Who comes to the training?

Men come from virtually every occupation, every religious, ethnic, racial, and socio-economic group. They have come from every state in the union, from Canada, and from as far away as New Zealand. The men range in age from sixteen to beyond seventy years. Professions include doctors, lawyers, salesmen, ministers, students, factory workers, university professors, corporate executives, policemen, and firemen. But all men who come to the weekend share a common understanding: that their lives **as men** lack adequate meaning and direction, and they want to do something about it.

Are there follow-up and auxiliary services?

There are ongoing follow-up support groups provided to integrate the learning. Where available, the weekly groups are led by trained facilitators. The **Spiritual Warrior** and **Shadow Warrior** are advanced trainings open only to New Warrior graduates. We are also affiliated with the **Woman Within** training program for women. Annual events include the **New Warrior Rendezvous** (spring), **Deer Camp** (autumn), and **Wolf Pack** (winter) every year in the American-Canadian Boundary Waters. A **Father-Son Weekend** is offered every July.

How is the New Warrior Training Adventure organization structured?

The New Warrior Network is a not-for-profit, international fraternal organization. The New Warrior trainings are conducted under the auspices of, and guidelines established by, the New Warrior Network. The trainings are conducted by the chapters in Milwaukee, Chicago, Minneapolis, San Diego, Tucson, and Rochester. Washington, D.C., Houston, Indianapolis, and Memphis may soon be organizing and running New Warrior Training events. New Warrior Network mission: **to empower men to a mission of service.**

Who is the New Warrior Network leadership?

The NWN elder council includes at least one man from each chapter. These are devoted men from a variety of professions including a business consultant, lawyer, industrial engineer, psychotherapist, physicist, and mediator. They are men best known by their life missions:

NEW WARRIOR™

Mission: ***to recreate human community***
Mission: ***to foster the development of spiritual masculinity***
Mission: ***to release the miracle within***
Mission: ***to empower and serve***
Mission: ***to empower men to authenticity***
Mission: ***to heal the despair of self-torture***
Mission: ***to create a safe planet through empowering men***

What's the "bottom line"?

The New Warrior Training is a safe container in which men can easily create a healthy new identity as men. As men define their missions as men of service they reclaim their lives as men. It is the giant step in a journey back toward honorable, self-respecting manhood.

The following are unsolicited comments from men who have taken the New Warrior journey.

On self-respect:
"I found out I'm more powerful and more loving than I thought I was."
"I feel stronger because of the clear identity of being a man. I'm more effective as a leader."
"It was great to celebrate the positive aspects of being a man."

On mission:
"The hard part was admitting what I want out of life. Once I did that, the passion, intuition, and power got it for me."
"For perhaps the first time in my life I feel a purpose. My life has meaning."

On obstacles:

"Since I learned to acknowledge and accept my feelings of anger and sadness, I have felt more love, joy, and passion. It makes my life worth living."

"I got in touch with the aggressive, angry, powerful, and wild part of myself. This was very hard for me."

On relationships:

"My lover-wife and I have a new relationship. It's based on mutual respect, deep intimacy, and shared passion."

"I feel a 'drawing toward' my wife during lovemaking . . . there was sublimated rage before. Nice change. I like it . . . and she really appreciates it!"

"It was the first time in twenty-eight years that my wife and I really got it together on all levels."

On parenting:

"For the first time in my life I am a real father for my children."

"I am very close with my previously estranged father."

"Taking a big step toward healing the issues with my dad was number one for me during the weekend."

"Learning to be there for my sons has brought them back into my life. It is priceless."

> "The real accomplishment [in life] is the art of being a warrior, which is the only way to balance the terror of being a man with the wonder of being a man."
>
> —Carlos Castaneda

On play:

"I feel more effective at home, at work, and especially at play. Play . . . that was something I didn't do enough of."

"I've never had so much fun over a weekend or any other time, till now."

On trust:

"It made me see myself as truly a man. It's made my friendships stronger and more open."

"I feel much more comfortable with and therefore better able to work with other men."

"I am no longer threatened by other men and treat them more as brothers than as competitors."

"Trusting my inner strength as a man, I can trust the strength of other men."

On self-exploration:

"When you've taken a look at yourself honestly, how risky can anything else be?"

For more information write to:
New Warrior Network
4125 W. Southland
Franklin, WI 53132

RECOMMENDED BOOKS AND TAPES

Over the years of doing men's work I've read lots of books, listened to lots of tapes, and formed some opinions about which ones are especially useful. I want to share that information with you. The following are personal reviews of what I consider the best men's information currently on the market. I borrowed some phrases from the Ally Press and Sounds True catalogs.

BOOKS

Iron John: A Book About Men
Robert Bly

An overnight bestseller Robert has been working on for a decade. This long-awaited book on male initiation and the role of the mentor is the result of Bly's work with men to discover their truths about masculinity. Iron John is the "Wild Man" who connects men to the earth and points the way toward developing what Bly calls the "inner warrior," whose task is not hostility and aggression but a steady resolve to know and defend what one loves. The rekindled model of masculinity will define a new era in relations between the sexes. (256 pages) Addison Wesley.

Men & Friendship
Stuart Miller

The best I've found on this topic, this book is a bold, sensitive, and courageous examination of the sorry state of friendships between men today. By detailing the difficulties and suggesting solutions, the author opens possibilities. A true friendship can make men stronger, wiser, and, so women say, better lovers. (206 pages) Gateway Books.

King, Warrior, Magician, Lover: Rediscovering the Archetypes of the Mature Masculine
Robert Moore and Douglas Gillette

This is a brilliant Jungian exploration of the question of what it means to be a man. I deeply value this presentation of these archetypes as ideals of authentic, revitalized masculinity not rooted in domination but in creativity and empowerment. I found the clear distinctions made between the immature and mature masculine within each of the four archetypes particularly useful. These archetypes are great self-identity tools in men's groups. (159 pages) Harper.

Knights Without Armor: A Practical Guide for Men in Quest of Masculine Soul

Aaron R. Kipnis, Ph.D.

Aaron combines his personal men's group experience (the "knights") with his knowledge of social and mythological perspective to offer us an amazing look at men's work today. He covers in detail the male wounds, authentic masculinity, our political, spiritual, and social selves. Aaron is a man with an astute eye on the process and, as his subtitle suggests, a splendid vision on who we are becoming. This is a highly readable, complete, and damn practical book. Enjoy and learn. (304 pages) Jeremy P. Tarcher Inc.

The Way of the Peaceful Warrior

Dan Millman

I admire Dan Millman as a man of integrity who lives what he teaches. Based loosely on his true story, this book has been inspirational for dozens of men I know. It is one of those books I hated to have end. I even read it again, out loud to my son when he was younger. He loved it, too. So journey with Dan as he learns how to live like a warrior guided by a powerful old warrior named Socrates. (210 pages) H. J. Kramer.

He: Understanding Masculine Psychology

Robert Johnson

What are some of the landmarks along the road to mature masculinity? The Jungian author follows the myth of the Fisher King, Parsifal, and the Grail Castle. (83 pages) HarperCollins.

Phallos: Sacred Image of the Masculine

Eugene Monick

This book, with its focus on the sacred phallos, is concerned with the archetypal basis of masculinity. As he examines the physical, mythological, and psychological manifestations of phallos, the author reintroduces an autonomous inner god, coequal with the maternal principles. A valuable book in dealing with body shame as it gives us back our cocks as a sacred part of us. (141 pages) Inner City Books.

Inside Out: Becoming My Own Man

Jed Diamond

I found this book to be a warm, funny, and outrageously open peek into a courageous man's life quest and exploration of his manhood. He looks deep into himself and tells his story with excitement. A pleasure to read. (184 pages) Fifth Wave Press. Also keep an eye out for Jed's new book, *The Warrior's Journey Home: Healing Men's Addictions*.

Flying Boy

John Lee

John is the father of the Austin Men's Center and of much fine men's work. This is his first and a very personal book. He was like many of us, what Bly calls the "Puer Aeternus," or eternal boy. Lee says, "If you fly away from commitments, responsibilities, intimacy, feelings, male friendships, and your own body, chances are you are a Flying Boy." Dad was absent and Mom tried to compensate. In the process, the boys rejected the masculine and overvalued the feminine. This is Lee's story of reclaiming his own masculinity. (122 pages) New Men's Press.

At My Father's Wedding: Reclaiming Our True Masculinity

John Lee

A passionate, heart-centered man who has truly done his own healing work, John shares his hard-won wisdom with us. In this clear and readable book he says that much of our pain and emptiness stem from the "Father Wound." He then suggests, often with his great storytelling, ways to heal our wounds. (201 pages) Bantam Books.

Healing the Shame that Binds Us

John Bradshaw

Although he does not allude to it directly, shame is a major part of our pain as men raised by women. I learned a lot from this book. In a brilliantly complete way, Bradshaw shows how "toxic shame" is the core problem in our codependencies, compulsions, and addictions. This book offers a clear, fresh look at shame as the core issue of societal and personal breakdown. He then provides an amazing overview of techniques for healing our shame. (244 pages) Health Communications.

Tending the Fire

Wayne Liebman

Building on Wayne's own mythology-oriented men's group, this excellent little book is authentic, honest, and a truly useful guide on working with ritual men's groups. I think of Wayne's book as a natural companion to my book; useful for men who have completed enough process. (54 pages) Ally Press.

The Book of Runes

Ralph Blum

This is the finest tool I've found to guide men out of their linear thinking habit. The runes are fun and can be stunning in offering an alternative-awareness experience. The book comes with a bag of "runes" (a selection of Celtic marked stones), which work like the I-Ching in providing "a mirror for the magic of our knowing selves." (151 pages) St. Martin's Press.

From the Hearts of Men

Yevrah Ornstein

Culled from his carefully fathered *The Men's Journal* comes this collection of men who speak with passion about their hopes, fears, dreams, hungers, needs, and about what they have to offer as men. Selections truly from the hearts of men. (330 pages) Harmonia Press.

Why Men Are the Way They Are

Warren Farrell

You have felt it, and you will still be amazed at the level of male bashing in our culture. Warren's well-researched book shows how the unhealthy prejudices about men are portrayed in the media from advertising to cartoons, all in graphic detail. This book is a major social exposé on how men's identity is currently being molded. (504 pages) McGraw-Hill.

To Be A Man: In Search of the Deep Masculine

Keith Thompson

Eighty-nine essays, spanning 100 years of classic and contemporary men's writing, considering the question, "What does it mean to be a man, to live with a deep awareness of a masculine sense of self?" (295 pages) Jeremy P. Tarcher, Inc.

Drama of the Gifted Child: The Search for the True Self

Alice Miller

This book blew my socks off when I read it in 1983. It is the single most powerful and clear book on narcissism, which afflicts most of us to some degree. Miller shows all too clearly how our authentic feelings were destroyed in childhood, leaving us with that four-year-old need to constantly be saying, "Me, me, me." (144 pages) Basic Books.

Mastery—A Technology for Excellence and Personal Evolution

Tim Piering

The basics of success, engineering an extraordinary life, going for it full-out, commitment and intention! Includes the fourteen principles from the "way of the warrior" and eight principles of the adventurer/healer. A detailed, practical, and spiritual guidebook. Could be a very useful tool in a committed men's group. (401 pages) Sun West Publishing Co.

Warriors of the Heart

Danaan Parry

"Our planet is crying out for men and women to own their power and to be positive agents of peaceful change." And this book is about learning to do just that. It is a joy to read and makes a challenging path a grand possibility. Find out what this remarkable man has to say! Also see audiotape by the same title. (206 pages) Sunstone Publications.

The Earthsteward's Handbook: A Guide to Healing Ourselves and Healing the Earth

Danaan Parry

If you are ready to get on a truly spiritual path of service, this book is the vehicle for making it happen. The Sevenfold Path of Peace is the step-by-step deepening of our awareness toward planetary transformation. This is a book to be savored. (157 pages) Sunstone Publications.

Love & Profits: The Art of Caring Leadership

James Autry

With love in his heart and poetry in his soul (and in his book) this seasoned Fortune 500 executive presents management as a truly humane possibility. Jim lives what he talks about. There are humor, honesty, pain, and passion in this book. If you are in business, read it. (213 pages) William Morrow.

Naked at Gender Gap: A Man's View of the War Between the Sexes

Asa Baber

This collection of Asa's "Men" columns from *Playboy* 1982–1992 is not to be missed. Hardy, feisty, funny, and gutsy as hell, Asa stands up for men in every possible way. And you don't have to wade through pages and pages of nubile curves just to read Asa's great stuff. (191 pages) Birch Lane Press.

What Men Won't Tell You *But* Women Need to Know

Bob Berkowitz

Who are the men of the 1990s? Bob will tell you in his own honest, sexy, witty, and sensible way. Playing with all the high (bald) spots from "Jerks R Us" to the "C-Word," Bob's humor will keep you reading to find out the next male secret. (177 pages) Avon Books.

The Code of the Warrior

Rick Fields

From the primary author of *Chop Wood, Carry Water* comes this fabulous book on true warriorship. I quote: "It is still an open question whether the human species will survive its own triumphant conquest of the planet. So we move from self to friend and lover, to family, band, clan, tribe, mother—and fatherland, brotherhood, sisterhood, and the human family—until we reach kinship with life itself, whose protection and care still springs from the code of the warrior within us all." This book gives us back the rich, socially functional traditions of warriors and the codes they embraced, often combining bravery and gentleness, self-mastery and a fierce compassion for others. (340 pages) Harper Perennial.

The Hazards of Being Male

Herb Goldberg

Written in 1975, this is the classic that stunned millions of men into waking up to the price we were paying for our male "privilege" and power. Herb has followed up with other men's books about every five years. You can trust it if "male" is in the title and Herb Goldberg is the author; it is worth the investment. (195 pages) Signet Books.

Fire in the Belly: On Being a Man

Sam Keen

Legend has it that Gorbachev was moved by some of the ideas contained in Sam's book, *Faces of the Enemy: Reflections of the Hostile Imagination*. A man who puts that kind of healing energy out in the world and has been in his own men's group for fifteen years is someone whom we can trust to guide us. It's a great, solid, and readable men's book. Don't miss Chapter 9, my favorite. (272 pages) Bantam Books.

A Choice of Heroes: The Changing Face of American Manhood

Mark Gerzon

As a passionate activist, Mark has led the way. So it figures that his visionary book has stood the test of time. For ten years it has been a gift to men everywhere as it boldly challenges the assumptions that have supported aggression and war. From John Wayne to the pope, our old heroes may not be serving us well. You can feel Mark as he guides us through his personal experiences to reveal the bigger picture, from an inside look at how LBJ's beliefs about manhood kept us in Vietnam to my favorite chapter, "The Lord," on how the constant use of male pronouns for God is a profound disservice to men. (280 pages) Houghton Mifflin.

AUDIO TAPES

Men and the Wound

Robert Bly

I sat in the front row of the 1985 Men's Conference for the keynote address by Robert Bly. With his characteristic irascible humor he presented the first two sections of the Iron John fairy tale. I wanted all the men I knew to hear it, so I got Robert's permission to edit and sell it. Many thousands of copies later, it is still a classic to enjoy. On the first side he tells the story straight through; he interprets it on the second side. He covers the wildman, initiation rites, male/female relationships, and the emotional wounds suffered between fathers and sons. (90 minutes)

Warriors of the Heart: How to Change the World We Live In

Danaan Parry

Ever since I read "We're Not Ready Yet, But Soon" (see Chapter 29), a passionate article on feeling healthy masculine power, Danaan Parry has been a hero of mine. A remarkable man whose work is about reclaiming our power to recreate our world gives a passionate message based on real-life experiences. He knows warriorship and suggests, "The job of the warrior is to make change happen." Those of us who have the courage to know ourselves, face our own fears, and then open up to new ideas and use them are "Warriors of the Heart." (90 minutes)

Healing the Masculine: An Archetypal View
Robert Moore

With his usual country-boy charm, Bob provides a rich and challenging overview of his brilliant insights into the four principal masculine archetypes: King, Warrior, Magician, and Lover, and the roles they play in a healthy male psyche. (90 minutes)

Off With the Rat's Head
Michael Meade

This classic tale of father-son conflict with commentary is a great introduction to Michael, who is the premier storyteller/drummer in the mythopoetic men's movement. (60 minutes)

The Naive Male
Robert Bly

The "devil's sooty brother" fairy tale is one of my favorites. In it we see the naive man as too trusting, vulnerable, passive, and ripe for the betrayal that may shock him from boyhood into manhood. This is a high-spirited, good-humored critique of the naively sensitive male. (90 minutes)

The Boy Who Married an Eagle: Myths and Stories About Male Individuation
Clarissa Pinkola-Estes

Can a woman talk about male issues? Yes, she can. She creates a brilliant and enjoyable journey in which she draws from a wealth of ancient myths and stories to weave a fascinating tapestry about the perils and processes of men setting themselves free. She is a gifted Jungian storyteller who touches on topics of integration of emotional life, where to begin inner work, what women want from men today, the search for balance, the sacred animal-man, and distractions of the cerebral, sexual, and spiritual appetites. (90 minutes)

Women Who Run with Wolves
Clarissa Pinkola-Estes

If, as you tell your wife/woman-friend about your reclaiming the wildman within, she says, "Hey, how about the wildwoman?" she'll love these tapes. And so will you. (2 x 90 minutes)

Fathering the Boy Within
James Sniechowski

Jim is a creative, high-integrity guy. This tape is a gentle, interactive guided meditation. So, if you are ready to "work," you will find this a very powerful tool to be used for healing the wounded child or recreating a boy loved by both mother and father. Perhaps this tape could be a catalyst for some great work in your men's group. (60 minutes)

The Great Self Within: Man and the Quest for Significance

Robert Moore and Michael Meade

It's about healthy grandiosity. Are you holding back? Feel the empowerment of Robert's insights into your psyche combined with Michael's mythological probes. These tapes are mandatory for any man who is a leader or who has an inkling toward leadership. (2 x 90 minutes)

VIDEOTAPE

A Gathering of Men

Robert Bly interviewed by Bill Moyers

As seen on your educational TV networks, this excellent overview of men's work today has touched millions of men. And as I suggested in Chapter 5, this tape would be a great way to introduce other men to the idea of a men's group. It is educational and fun to watch. Most men are moved by this tape. (60 minutes)

MEN'S AWARENESS CATALOGUE

These recommended books and tapes can be ordered through the:

Men's Awareness Catalogue
8120 S. 68th St.
Franklin, WI 53132

Write for free copy of the catalogue and price list.

About the Author

Bill Kauth, M.S., psychotherapist and counselor to business executives, has been active in the men's movement for twenty years, and is cofounder of The New Warrior Training Adventure™, one of the oldest and most respected men's initiation organizations, with branches in Chicago, Houston, Memphis, Minneapolis, Washington, D.C., San Diego, and many other cities, including his hometown of Milwaukee.

© LotterMoser 1991